A FIELD GUIDE TO THE LITTLE PEOPLE

A field Guide to the Little people

Nancy Arrowsmith
with George Moorse

ILLUSTRATED BY
heinz edelmann

CALLIGRAPHY BY
Kevin Reilly

HILL AND WANG · NEW YORK
A division of Farrar, Straus and Giroux

Text © Nancy Arrowsmith, 1977
Illustrations © Heinz Edelmann, 1977
Calligraphy and typography © Macmillan London Limited, 1977
All rights reserved

Calligraphy by Kevin Reilly

ISBN 0-8090-4450-1

Printed in the United States of America
Second printing, 1978

Library of Congress Cataloging in Publication Data
Arrowsmith, Nancy.
  A field guide to the Little People.
  Bibliography: p.
  Includes index.
  1. Fairies. 2. Folk-lore—Europe.
  I. Moorse, George. joint author. II. Title.
GR549.A76   1977   398'.45   77-13706

CONTENTS

CONTENTS

... all nature is full of invisible people ... some of these are ugly or grotesque, some wicked or foolish, many beautiful beyond any one we have ever seen, and ... the beautiful are not far away when we are walking in pleasant and quiet places.

W. B. Yeats, *Mythologies*

AUTHOR'S NOTE

Elf is a generic term for all Little People, and is the term most commonly used in this book. *Sprite* too is a generic term for all Little People. *Spirit* is used to refer to wood spirits, water spirits, nature spirits, etc.; it has nothing to do with spiritualism. The term *fairy* is avoided in the book because it has been so often misused, for example in 'fairy tale' and to mean homosexual, and so on. Elves of Celtic origin are called *Faeries*, and the term is used as a specific name. *Dwarf* is a generic name usually applied to Dark Elves; it is never used in reference to Light Elves.

Other terms such as *imp*, *goblin*, *wight*, etc., are used rarely in the book. There are also hundreds of euphemistic names for the Little People: the Fair Folk, the Good Folk, the Forgetful Folk, the Good Neighbours from the Sunset Land, the Hidden Folk, the Night Folk, Them, the Little Darlings, Mother's Blessing, the Lovers, etc.

A name in SMALL CAPITALS indicates a separate entry for the species concerned. An asterisk (*) indicates a note at the back of the book, while superior numbers indicate footnotes. The sources of the stories will also be found among the notes at the back, where they are identified by opening and closing phrases.

NANCY ARROWSMITH

INTRODUCTION

FROM the beginning of recorded history the Little People have held an important position in the folk cultures of the world. At one time, when each tree had a name, when every deer was recognized, they grew and thrived in the country and in small villages where farmers worked the land like their fathers before them. Known and called by name, they were numerous and very powerful, and played a large role in everyday life.

In those times, men were not considered the supreme rulers of our planet. The world was peopled not only with humans and animals but also with giants, gods, monsters, ghosts, spirits and elves, many of them the equals of men in cunning, strength and power. With the coming of Christianity, belief in spirits and 'false' gods was discouraged; but despite this official disapproval, many of the old traditions lived on, slightly changed to suit the new times. Until a few centuries ago, elves still held a position in the folklore of Europe second only to the Devil and Christ.

Elves are nature spirits, Mother Nature's children. They are spritely, sad, vengeful, morose, friendly, fun-loving and hateful in turn, as many-sided as nature herself – psychic fauna who take many forms, appearing as iridescent beauties or as crippled old men with hunchbacks, as goats, caterpillars, cats, stones, plants or even gusts of wind. They range in height from those the size of a man to those so small that they can hide under a blade of grass. Elves are 'more unstable and transmutative in their shapes and natures, and are not so clearly distinguishable from each other'* as men or animals. They are not generally bound by the material precepts of our existence, often having the ability to travel instantaneously through the dimensions and vanish altogether.

Because of these abilities and characteristics, it has always been a difficult matter for humans to see elves. Children, poets, seers, healers, those gifted with second sight, men and women at peace with and in tune with their natural surroundings have historically been those most likely to enter into contact with the Little People.

Reports of such encounters were first transmitted orally by storytellers, wise men and women, priests, witches, servants and poets. Hallucinogenic or poisonous drugs, complicated rites of initiation and experience were once used to facilitate communication with elves and other fantastic beings, but all accounts agree that the main pre-requisite to seeing the elves is an emotional affinity or a 'blood-relationship' with them. Relationships (sexual or otherwise) with elves are always reported as being difficult to maintain, and both parties are usually bound by a great number of taboos.

It is only in the last century that detailed word-for-word written accounts of the earlier oral reports have been set down and preserved. These accounts have formed my basic research sources. I have not used literary sources because, in my opinion, the imagination and fancy of writers often alter or confuse the facts of elf-existence as it has been recognized in folk belief for centuries. (Hobbits, for example, are not included because there have been no reports of Hobbit-sightings to date.)

Now that the Little People have retreated before man, his noisy cities and polluted streams, we find it harder still to come into contact with them, although they can sometimes be discovered in the country, in deserted houses, on mountain-tops, in rivers and in open fields. Most reports of modern sightings are so fragmentary as to be easily forgotten, and those who do actually encounter the elves are led to believe that their experience was just a fancy, a flight of the imagination, an aberration. This book is an attempt to treat a definite body of folk-information in a scientific manner by codifying reports of sightings and presenting them clearly to the modern reading public. The elves are here spoken of as belonging to species, genera and families, and their identifying characteristics and habitats are given, along with stories of their activities and dealings with men. I hope both to have simplified the task of identifying the elves of Europe and to have created a larger interest in them by opening the reader's eyes to the possibility of their actual existence in our day and age.

One of my most difficult tasks has been that of sifting older, more believable and more complete versions of folk tales and oral reports from newer, Christianized or garbled versions. If what modern folklore theoreticians say is true, that the background and origin of most folk tales can be found in the Stone Age (!), and because of the Little People's 'elusive and transmutative' natures, it is obvious that codification and classification is at best problematic. Any system is by necessity incomplete and liable to suffer from contradictions, and the writer is often forced to rely on intuition and luck as well as on endless examinations of the material, careful historical reconstructions, exercises in logic and linguistics, categorization and sub-classification.

I have however been able to distinguish three separate groups of elves from the confusion and have used this division as the organizational backbone of the book.

Light Elves are masters at shape-changing and can travel through the four known dimensions. Their beauty is often evanescent, like that of the butterfly. They are among the best-natured Little People, but are unfortunately less often seen by humans than the Dark or Dusky Elves.

The *Dark Elves*, like caterpillars, make their homes in the earth and their skin reflects its colours: grey, brown, red and black. They occasionally live in human houses, but always prefer dark corners and only appear at noon or late at night.

The *Dusky Elves* are by far the most numerous. They are tied to their environment and their life is defined by laws of time, space and place. Because of these limitations, they can be more easily recognized by humans, hence the large role they play in this book. One can compare them to the butterfly in its chrysalid stage, a pupa bound by silken threads to its environment. Dusky Elves take great pains to shield themselves from foreign interference and rarely travel far from their native tree, herb, brook, mound or pond.

Although it has been fairly easy to separate the elves into these three categories, precise classification into species and families has proved more difficult. For example, Changelings are usually referred to as Changelings, regardless of the elf-species to which they belong. Changelings exchanged for humans by the Irish SIDHE bear the same name as those of the GWAGGED ANNWN, and the German Stille Volk and Moosweibchen Changelings are both called Wechselbälge. To further complicate matters, an extremely large number of popular names exist for each species of elf, while the names SKOGSRÅ, Thusser, MOUND FOLK and Trolls may all be found to designate the same elves in accounts from varying times and authors.

Another problem has been the unevenness of distribution: Ireland, for example, has more recorded folk tales per inhabitant than any other country in Europe, while Spanish records are so sketchy that it is difficult to find any references at all. In many countries, especially the Slavic ones, the information and knowledge contained in folk tales have only rarely been compiled, translated, or presented to the West.

Despite confusion over naming and classification, accounts of elf sightings seem to suggest distinct patterns. From the great body of information about them, one can extract a general picture of what an elf is, apart from all variations in size, nature and appearance.

Elves are extremely old beings, possessing many traits and characteristics in common with the older European peoples (Lapps, Celts, Teutons, etc.). In order to gain power over them, humans have only to make them reveal their age, which is, in every case, venerable. In keeping with their age, elves are very conservative. They distrust iron and steel, religion, industrialization; they are not fond of humans who follow new ways, even going to the extreme of tabooing the use of salt and spices in the preparation of food. They are often incapable of counting and do not know the names of the days of the week.

Some elves have hollow backs: they are never quite corporeal in our world. Elf-women often have long drooping breasts, like many animals, and are capable of working in the fields and at the same time giving suck to baskets of children on their backs, an arrangement indicating their extreme fecundity. Other elves have human appearance, sometimes with the exception of animal feet, ears, skin or teeth. Both elf-men and elf-women dress in old-fashioned peasant clothes, wear the colours of magic, red and green, or go naked. Materialism and material things are not respected by the Little People, to the great discomfiture of many humans.

In our time it may seem irrelevant to speak of old pagan beliefs, of elves and beings of folklore. But is there not some truth in the old stories? In our endless search for a more modern form of life, we have rejected the harsher existence of the village for that of the city, have forgotten the names of the elves and have disfigured the earth with our tools and machinery. We have moved from city to city in search of profit and with each move have grown less sensitive to the nuances of nature. We no longer have the ability to see elves with our children's or seers' eyes. Instead we read of the LEPRECHAUN and laugh at the simplicity of people who can still believe in him. This book was written for people who want to rediscover elves – the majestic, cruel, beautiful and irrepressible elves of our forefathers.

LIGHT
ELVES

ALVEN

THE Dutch *Alven* are the most representative species of Light Elves. Their bodies are so insubstantial to our eyes that we usually call them invisible. They can travel through the air with the same ease with which they cross rivers and streams, gliding quietly through the currents.

The Alven should never be taken lightly. Their bodies may look weak, but their power is awesome. They control many bodies of water, including the fabled River Elbe. Their power is at its strongest at night, when they wake from their sleep and come to land to do mischief and greet friends. They then care for their favourite plants, night wort and elf-leaf, watering and strengthening them against the coming day. Their attachment to these plants is so strong that they will sicken or kill cattle and humans who touch them.

Identification: Very few detailed descriptions of the Alven exist because of their translucent, almost transparent bodies. To further complicate things, the Alven are shape-changers and can shrink to minuscule size, only to then grow and spread into gorgeous monsters which cover half of the morning sky.

Habitat: The Dutch Alven live in ponds in which there are no fish, or under small mounds called Alvinnen hills. They travel with the wind and through water inside air bubbles or broken eggshells.

Sidhe

THE Faeries are one of the most populous species of European Little People. The word 'fairy' has been continually misused and misapplied throughout the English-speaking world, but the Faeries are still a people of great power in Ireland. They are the descendants of the original Irish, the Tuatha dé Danaan. Those with the closest ties to the Tuatha are called the *Sidhe* (pronounced 'Shee') or Daoine Sidhe. They are the aristocrats of Faerie, very beautiful and of great size, great age and even greater power. Their music is a joy to listen to and their Queen, Maeve, is of such beauty that it is dangerous for humans to look at her. The only one who rivals her power is the Fool, Amadán-na-Briona, the most dreaded individual in Faerie. As the Irish put it, 'to meet the Amadán is to be in prison for ever'.*

The Sidhe live a very domestic life if left undisturbed, caring for their animals, drinking whisky, borrowing milk and meal. But if they are molested or if any of their taboos are broken, they will react with great violence. Their touch alone can sicken or madden a human and their elf-arrows cause instant paralysis or death. People they fancy are kidnapped and made to act as slaves or concubines inside their hills. Even a short stay with the Faeries changes humans completely and they return to Earth as madmen, seers, healers or prophets.

There are many ways to avoid angering the Faeries. Even more numerous are the means of protecting oneself against them. A few of the most important should always be kept in mind: never eat faerie food but, on the other hand, never forget to leave them an offering of food and water, or some milk, potatoes, tobacco or whiskey. If milk is spilled, 'there's someone the better for it',* and those who don't cry over the fact win the approval of the Faeries. Slovenly people are despised by the Faeries, and for that reason the house, and especially the fireplace, should be swept early and then all the ashes and rubbish thrown out well before dark.

One should avoid contact with the Sidhe while they are at their strongest: on the moving-days of 1 May and Hallowe'en when they move to their summer or winter homes, during the month of May, at twilight, before sunrise and at noon. One should never walk inside faerie circles or over faerie hills and under no circumstances try to build a house there. One should always tip one's hat when passing a dust devil, and never turn around to look back at a faery. Cutting down a thorn bush or leaving something on a faerie path invites disaster, and those who praise a person without saying 'God bless him' make it possible for the faeries to take him to their world.

The most effective protection against the Faeries is iron, but salt and religious objects may also be used. A four-leaved clover in one's hat makes it possible to see the Faeries.

Identification: The Sidhe are thin, up to six feet in height, handsome and young-looking despite their great age. Their forms are shadowy, and they can only fully materialize in the presence of a human. Even their beauty is that of another world. Their skin is soft, their hair long and flowing, their clothes blindingly white. Their voices are sweet and seductive and their bagpiping unrivalled.

There are several individuals among the Irish Faeries: Willy Rua, who gets the first drops of each new batch of whiskey; the Stroke Lad, who comes at the end of every faerie procession; and the ruthlessly seductive Lhiannan-Sidhe who destroys men with her beauty.

Habitat: The Sidhe live under faerie hills, although there are stories of fantastic floating islands peopled only by the most beautiful Faeries.

A woman returned to her old house after seven years' absence. She had been taken by the Faeries and had danced with them so long that her toes were worn away.

As she was gathering nuts in the forest, a girl heard music of a kind different from any she had ever known. It warmed her heart and made her forget the half-gathered nuts lying beneath the tree. The soft whisper of the wind was loud in comparison with this music, and she thought of things far away and of rivers flowing slowly to the sea, until twilight darkened around her and she could hear no more.

She told her mother of the music and left even earlier the next day for the woods. She stood there beneath the nut tree, listening until the last echoes of the song had faded and the stars glittered in the night. She went again the next day to listen and the music overwhelmed her and followed her home, filling her room with its magic. Then suddenly it stopped. When the girl emerged from her room, her mother asked her about the strange sounds.

'There was no music, Mother. You must have imagined it.'

With a doubtful shake of her head, the mother turned back to her work and said no more about it. The next day she found her daughter dead in bed. When the neighbours came to the wake, they found a hag with long teeth in her place. She was so old and so wrinkled that she could have been a hundred. That night the music was heard again. The mother saw flashing coloured lights outside every window and heard for the last time the music of the pipers who had taken her daughter away.

A young boy stood on the shore looking out to sea, and saw two flights of 'Them' sweeping over a fishing-boat, flying so fast and low that the water was pushed away on either side, showing the sand beneath. The poor fisherman made little headway as They swept at him again and again, cheering and laughing, enjoying Their sport. As They rose from the boat, They were like a great cloud of dust. Then the boy saw Their faces, always laughing, and changing colour at every turn.

A small shepherd's cottage had earned the reputation of being haunted. All who moved there died soon afterwards. Even the dogs that slept by the fire vanished mysteriously. The house stood empty for many years, for no one dared to stay there. Finally a poor woman decided to give it a try. She had no place to go and thought even a haunted house better than no house at all.

The first day, nothing happened, and there were no incidents on the second. The woman was feeling quite proud of herself when a knock came at the door. She opened and a tall beautiful lady asked, 'Excuse me, may I borrow some oatmeal?'

The woman generously gave the stranger what she had, and refused to take anything in return when the Faery came a few days later to repay her debt. 'The oats have gone to a good use, I dare say. I won't need them any more.'

'As long as you don't open the back door, then,' the faerie lady replied, 'you can live here as long as you like. I promise that we won't bother you.'

The woman warmly thanked the Faery, and lived peaceably in the house for the rest of her life. The Faeries moved their path from its original place outside her door and, true to their word, never bothered her again.

FYLGIAR

IN ICELAND, a child born with a caul, or membrane, over his head is considered very lucky. The caul, in Icelandic 'fylgia', is carefully saved and buried under the threshold. The child's mother must then walk over the buried fylgia and her baby will be blessed in later life with a lucky attendant spirit. In both Iceland and Norway, this sprite is called a *Fylgia*. It follows its master wherever he goes, taking the form of his totem animal, or acting as his double. Because Fylgiar always shadow their masters, it is considered extremely impolite to shut a door quickly behind a person. The Fylgia might then be shut outside the room, unable to help his master. Although invisible, the Fylgia makes its presence known before the arrival of visitors by knocking and banging, opening doors and shuffling its feet in the hall. It only becomes visible to its master shortly before his death, warning him of the coming event. A bloody Fylgia will mean a violent death for the master; a quiet Fylgia a more peaceful end.

Identification: Fylgiar can only be seen by their masters on the point of death and by those gifted with second sight. A man can discover what animal form his Fylgia takes by a simple ritual. He should wrap a knife in a napkin and hold it high, repeating the names of all the animals he knows. When he comes to the name of his totem animal, the knife will drop from the napkin. Among other names for the Fylgia: in Iceland, Forynia and Hamingia; in Norway: Folgie, Vardögl, Vardygr, Vardivil, Vardöiel and Ham.

Habitat: The Fylgiar keep an invisible one or two steps behind their masters and sleep near them at night. They are most often heard of in Iceland and Norway.

Clumsy Thorsten stumbled on entering the room. 'Damn!'
The old man sitting in the corner began to shake with suppressed laughter.

'What the hell is so funny?' the boy yelled. 'Laughing like a fool just because someone stumbles! Haven't you got anything better to do?'

'Don't be so hasty, boy, with your anger. I wasn't laughing at your stumbling, I was laughing at what you can't see. You were in such a hurry to come into the room that you fell over your Fylgia. Have you ever seen anyone trip on a furry white bear cub? I can assure you, it's quite a sight.'

ellefolk

ALTHOUGH the *Ellefolk* are often classed as Trolls, they have little in common with their relatives the MOUND FOLK or the SKOGSRÅ. They are Light Elves, are not daybound and can travel with great ease through air, fire, wood, water and stone. The females ride sunbeams through keyholes while the males prefer to sit on the edges of the moors, basking in the morning sunlight. Both males and females can foretell the future and are the guardians of ancient secrets. But their favourite occupation by far is dancing. On moonlit nights, they can often be seen, weaving patterns of incredible complexity, tirelessly celebrating to the delicate music of stringed instruments. The grass grows better where they have danced and rich circles of green blossom under their feet. They are such masters of the musical arts that a few notes on one of their instruments are enough to make a human lose his reason.

Because of their power over all things natural and the great beauty and strength of their lives, it is very dangerous for humans to come into contact with them. A single whiff of their breath can cause sickness and even death. A man who sees one of their females through a knot in a tree will leave his wife and home in order to join her. Women should avoid disturbing the Ellemen at their sunbathing, or they will be lured into the realm of the Ellefolk. Cows should not graze where these elves have passed, or they will sicken and join the large elfin herds. But the magic of the elfin dance remains the most dangerous temptation for those of our world. Men who have stepped inside their circles and felt the whirling vibrations of their madness can find no safe haven on earth.

Identification: Although the Ellefolk are usually considered Danish elves, the name can also be applied to the similar Swedish (called Elfor) and Norwegian sprites.

The female Ellefolk are young, beautiful and seductive, but have a hollow back. Their breasts are long and drooping, their hair loose and blonde. Their height is a little above four feet and their voices are soft and gentle.

The male Ellefolk are shorter than the females, and wear broad-brimmed hats. The Danish and Swedish Ellemen are most often seen as old men, the Norwegian as naked young boys.

Habitat: The Ellefolk live in ellemoors, next to rivers, under hills and in marshes. Their homes can be seen only once by humans and then vanish, never to be found again. Those who have seen the Ellefolk talk of fabulous gardens hidden in the moss at the edge of forests. The Ellefolk and Elfor live in Denmark, Sweden and Norway.

The cows were grazing, the sun shone high overhead, and the herdsman had little work. He tried to overcome his sleepiness and thought of what he had to do at home. A visit to his

The Ellefolk

girlfriend . . . a walk around town in his new clothes . . . an evening with his friends. . . . He was so absorbed in these daydreams that he didn't notice the beautiful girl who had sat down right beside him.

'You look hungry,' she said in a sultry voice. 'Come, I'll give you something to drink. Take a suck, *if* you dare.'

The young man was so bewildered by the girl and by her voice that at first he didn't notice what she was asking him to do.

'Come on, don't be afraid,' she cooed.

It was only then that the cowherd saw her naked breast.

'Just one drink!' she coaxed at the back of his mind. Before he had time to think, the boy was in her arms and her nipple was in his mouth. He stayed there for an eternity, in which he remembered snatches of conversations, days of love, and sweet, sweet songs. It was only slowly that he returned to himself and stumbled into the safety of his father's house.

He could not answer the anxious questions of his parents, who immediately assumed that he had been bewitched. His father forced him to eat a piece of raw meat before he fell into a coma that lasted three days.

Maybe the meat saved his life, but it did not save his mind. When he awoke, he could only dream of elfin folk and vague twists of half-forgotten visions.

WIND FOLLETTI

ALL FOLLETTI travel in wind twirls, or as they are known in Italy 'knots of wind'. It is usually the FOLLETTO's fault when the wind turns destructive and unleashes rain and snow, wrecking crops and flooding houses. Many winds get their names from the FOLLETTI who travel in them and many FOLLETTI are named after the winds they ride.

However, certain FOLLETTI occupy themselves solely with winds and the weather. They are most numerous and dangerous in Sicily, which has one of the most violent climates in the Mediterranean. The Macinghe are *Wind Folletti* who violate women. The Mazzamarieddu or Ammazzamareddu only travel when they have seen the blood of an assassinated man. They are responsible for earthquakes as well as wind and snowstorms. Their special enemies are the saints Filippo and Giacomo, with whom they fight every year. If the wind begins to blow on the saints' feast day, the farmers know that the Mazzamarieddu are winning and chew as much garlic as they can to drive the FOLLETTI away.

In Sardinia, wind twirls are caused by the Sumascazzo, who predicts misfortunes. In Friuli, the Grandinili, or 'little hail people', bring the hail, and can only be driven away by the sound of church bells. The Mazzamarelle are known in Calabria, Lazio and Abruzzo under various names. In Abruzzo, they take the form of little boys with castanets and silk hats who travel in whirlwinds and bang about in houses. The northern Italian Basadone ('woman-kisser') rides the noonday breeze and steals kisses as he passes by. He is a lord and his subjects are responsible for dust twirls seen in the fields.

Identification: The Wind Folletti are about the same size as the normal FOLLETTI, but are almost always invisible. The Abruzzo Mazzamarelle is about two feet high and wears a silk hat with flowers. He carries castanets. At times he also takes the form of a grasshopper.

Habitat: The Wind Folletti are known throughout Italy.

cahice ladies

THE Fainen, Weisse Frauen and Sibille of northern Europe fulfil many of the same functions as the local fertility elves of southern Europe such as the FATE, FÉES, Hadas and Korrigans. Like the Korrigans and FÉES, they have also been associated with the old pagan priestesses. Either because they cannot adjust to the ways of modern man, or because they are slowly dying off, the *White Ladies* have not been seen often in this century. They are, in fact, so rarely seen that they are confused with ghosts and wood-women.

The White Women are helpful and generous towards humans. They can help travellers find the right road, change flowers and stones into precious amulets, aid women in childbirth, show men veins of gold and silver, make cows produce more milk, foretell the future, lessen the fury of storms and give many useful presents. Despite their generous natures, they can be easily angered by vicious, cruel or ungrateful men, and punish them with extreme severity.

Identification: The White Ladies have in recent years become very rare. The Tirolean Fainen can only be seen when they kiss a child, by those born on a Sunday or those with an elf talisman. They then materialize in the form of strikingly beautiful young women with long blonde hair and flimsy white gowns.

Habitat: The Fainen, Weisse Frauen and Sibille live in Germany, Austria, Holland and parts of Denmark. The Weisse Frauen are usually seen near old castles, and the Sibille haunt linden trees and sacred groves. The Dutch Witte Juffern prefer to live in caves close to small towns.

A White Lady

A boy was lucky enough to find an unusual playmate, high in the mountains. She was unlike any of the other girls, very beautiful, with shining white clothes, soft blue eyes and golden hair, garlanded with a crown of gentians and edelweiss.

The two played happily all day. Then the strange girl had to leave and left her playmate a few stones as a goodbye present. The boy was delighted, for the stones sparkled with an almost blinding light. But when he brought them indoors that evening, they lost their glint and sparkle and turned the dull, lustreless colour of raw gold.

Years went by, and the boy grew into a young man. His golden treasure was soon spent on clothes and drink, and he turned into a woman-chaser. As luck would have it, he chose to seduce a girl at the same place where he had once met the blue-eyed Fai. He told the girl that he loved her, but had no intention of marrying her or ever seeing her again.

The Fai had not interfered in the young man's life since their first meeting. But she could not act as a witness to his cruelty now. She threw him off a cliff, and slapped the girl so hard that a red welt rose on her face, which she kept until the day of her death. When the girl's children were born, they also carried the same mark, as well as their children and their children's children. The family of the young man did not escape the Fai's wrath as easily. All the males, boys, men and grandfathers, died within the same year.

Dames Vertes

ORIGINALLY forest elves, the *Dames Vertes* have lately been seen close to human habitations. At one time, they lived together in small groups in the forest and led men astray, destroying them with the violence of their emotions and the exuberance of their lovemaking. The Dames Vertes were later seen at the edge of the woods, teasing travellers, laughing at young people and dangling strangers by their hair over waterfalls. Then they became friends with the wind and travelled over the ripening grain, breathing life into the seed with every step. They appeared before fires, visiting the fields and orchards with their haunting presence.

Through their long association with the wind, the Dames Vertes have become more and more ethereal until, at the present time, they are sometimes referred to as revenants, or visitors from another world. It cannot be denied that the winds of the Dames Vertes smell of earth and mould and death, but to refer to them as 'ghosts' is far from correct. Their nature, however ethereal, remains that of a life-giving, greening force, like the warm wind that melts the winter's snows.

Identification: The Dames Vertes are tall, beautiful and extremely seductive, and dress in green tunics. Very rarely seen in their natural forms, they are usually invisible, walking so gracefully and lightly over a field that the only sign of their passage is a slight ripple in the grass.

Habitat: The Dames Vertes live in thickly wooded areas in eastern France, at the edge of meadows, in forest caves, near waterfalls and springs, and on the slopes that lead to fishponds. They have occasionally been known to work inside houses. During rainy weather, they can be found behind trees or overhanging vines.

ꟷ WILL O' THE WISP

PHOSPHORESCENT flames or lights seen in swamps and other deserted places have long puzzled scientists. But folk belief has been able to explain them for many years. The *Will-o'-the-Wisp* are no ordinary lights, but ones which show us Elfland, flashing from its borders as lightning before a storm. Many humans find these lights hypnotizing and will follow them wherever they lead, into bogs and marshes or over cliffs.

The flames are not elves, but lights carried by elves. These elves are animated by the souls of men, women and children. As such, they come closer to being 'ghosts' than any other elves. They still remember their lives on Earth, and have not been completely welcomed into the elfin world. Because of their insecurity, they are worried about the future, continually asking men and elves what will become of them. On the whole, their relationship with men is good, for they haven't forgotten the ways of their old world and still have compassion for its inhabitants.

Identification: The Will-o'-the-Wisp take a variety of forms. In Russia, still-born and unbaptized children are stolen after their death by the RUSALKY and taken to live in their underwater homes. The English and Scottish Spunkies are also the souls of unbaptized children. The souls of boundary-stone movers, usurers and swindlers become the Will-o'-the-Wisp in England, while the Italian Fuochi Fatui are said to be souls in Purgatory. The Swedish Lygte Men are the souls of landmark movers as are the German Luchtenmannekens.

When the Will-o'-the-Wisp show themselves at sea, Catholics call them St Elmo's Fire, but more superstitious sailors call

The Will-o'-the-Wisp

them the souls of the drowned. The Northern Lights are also thought to be elves dancing at night. In Scotland, they are known as the Nimble Men or the Merry Dancers, and in some sections of France as the Chèvres Dansantes or dancing goats.

Among the many other names for the Will-o'-the-Wisp: in Latin, Ignis Fatuus; in Sardinia, Candelas; in Scandinavia, Lyktgubbe or Irrbloss; in Germany, Huckepoten, Irrlichter or Heerwische; in Czechoslovakia, Swetylko; in Wales, Ellylldan; in France, Tan Noz, Éclaireux, Annequins, Fioles, Loume-rottes and Culards; and in England, Elf Fire, Kit-with-the-Canstick, Jack o' Lanthorn, Joan-in-the-Wad and Hob-and-his-Lanthorn.

Habitat: The Will-o'-the-Wisp are known throughout Europe and can be met at sea or on land. They most often show themselves in late summer, autumn and winter and prefer to live in damp places such as swamps, on moors or in the vicinity of graveyards. They are rarely seen when the weather is sunny, but often on heavy overcast days.

DARK
ELVES

KNOCKERS

Knockers are extremely helpful spirits who make their homes inside mines and quarries. They are skilful and industrious miners who know the location of every ore-bearing vein in Europe. They can sometimes even be heard hammering and knocking in deep abandoned tunnels. It is from this endless knocking and hammering that they have received their name.

The Knockers not only know of the existence of veins of ore, but also tell their favourites where they can be found. In most sections of Europe, it is considered extremely lucky to hear the Knockers at their work, and many miners have, in fact, discovered rich pockets of silver, gold, tin or lead by following the sound of tiny elfin pickaxes. The Knockers also serve as warning spirits: when disaster is about to strike, they can be heard knocking loudly and erratically, or one of them may be seen sitting on the sick litter at the entrance to the shaft, moaning and rubbing his head. In Bohemia, when a miner is about to die, the Knockers warn his relatives by coming to his house at night and knocking loudly until morning.

In return for their kindnesses and the luck they bring, the little miners should be fed as regularly as possible: a small offering left in their favourite corner of the mine, a doughnut presented to them at the mine entrance. In Istria, they receive gifts of clothing once or twice a year and are very upset if they are forgotten. The two things the Knockers despise most are whistling and swearing. Laughing and singing are perfectly acceptable, but whistling can often move the normally peaceful Knockers into such fits of rage that they are capable of causing cave-ins, or twisting men's heads right off their shoulders.

Identification: The mine elves, besides the common name of Knockers, also have strictly local names. In Wales they are called Coblynau, in Austria Schacht-Zwergen or 'shaft dwarfs', in Germany Berg-Mönche ('mountain monks') or Meister Hämmerlinge ('master hammerlings'), in France Gommes and in Scotland Black Dwarfs. They range in size from one and a half to three feet high, dress in miners' clothes and leather aprons, carry tiny picks, and are most often seen on Sundays and holidays.

Habitat: Stories of the Knockers are told in most European mining communities. The Cornish miners say the Knockers date from Roman times, and the Italians spoke of them in the early Middle Ages. They are well-known in Wales, Scotland, Germany, Yugoslavia, Romania and Austria. Although certain house spirits are also called Knockerlings, they cannot be properly called Knockers but should instead be considered POLTERSPRITES. Knockers are strictly mine spirits.

'**B**e careful! Rocks are falling!'

'Someone is *throwing* them at us!'

Angered by this sudden interruption of their work, three miners shoved their cart back over the bridge to find out what was happening. There in front of them stood a tiny mountain dwarf dressed in miner's clothes, with a rock in his hand.

'What do you think you're doing?' shouted the oldest. 'If you Knockers weren't so strong, I'd beat the living daylights out of you!'

Before the man could say anything else, a loud rumble echoed through the mine. Looking back, the miners saw the bridge crumble and fall apart. Of the Knocker there was no sign, but the miners thanked him gratefully for their escape.

A Knocker

In the last century, miners were poorly paid and often had to send their children underground to increase their income. Even then it was hard to keep the family fed.

It was a boy's first trip into the mine. His father had always told him stories about it and the Mountain Monk who lived in it, but this was the first time he had actually experienced it for himself. The boy's excitement waned as the day wore on and the work grew harder and harder. He began to feel hungry, tired and thirsty. Just then he saw a friend tuck a parcel into a niche in the wall. Waiting until his friend had left, he unwrapped the paper and greedily gobbled the muffin he found inside.

It was only after he had eaten the last crumb that he remembered his father's stories of the offerings of food for the Mountain Monk. By then it was too late: the Mountain Monk was already behind him. That evening, the boy was found dead, his head twisted off.

Erdluitle

THE *Erdluitle* or 'earth folk' all have one thing in common: they are extremely reluctant to show their feet to humans. Whether their motivation is simple shyness or whether they do not want to reveal the source of their power is not clear. The only certainty is that the Erdluitle are of older ancestry than human beings and have more knowledge of the secret powers of nature.

The Erdluitle have great control over the weather. They are closely related to the Ice and Fog Mannikins and have many of the same skills. They can cause storms, floods and avalanches, and tell farmers when the time is right for planting. The land produces more where they have held a dance. All herd and pasture animals come under their protection, as do chamois and mountain game. They know the secret of making chamois-milk cheese and can turn green leaves into gold and diamonds. The Erdweibchen ('earthwives') are good spinners and often work in farmers' houses. They bring luck if allowed to hold their weddings indoors or if the mistress of the house helps them in childbirth.

Unfortunately, relationships between humans and Erdluitle have been deteriorating in the last few years, just as the relationship between humans and Nature has been deteriorating. Although the Erdweibchen influence all phases of a farmer's life, men have nonetheless chosen to ridicule and persecute them instead of giving them the respect they deserve. As a result, very few Erdluitle are left in Switzerland and, despite new farming machinery, it is becoming less and less profitable for individual farmers to work the land.

Identification: The Erdluitle are known under a variety of names. The males of the species are called Härdmandlene, Gotwergi, Heidenmanndli or Bergmanli, and in northern Italy, Guriuz. The females are called Erdbibberli, Heidenweibchen, Erdweibchen or Herdweibchen. Swiss Erdluitle-changelings are called Chrügeli.

The Erdluitle are gregarious. They are about one and a half to three feet high, or the size of a seven-year-old child. Their skin is earth-coloured. The young Erdluitle have dark hair, the old white. They wear red or black cloaks or hoods over green, blue or grey smocks. Their clothes are unusually long so that their goose or duck feet won't show. Some of them, in addition to goose feet, have animal ears. Their favourite foods are roots, berries, peas and pork.

Habitat: The Erdluitle are a Swiss and northern Italian sub-species of dwarf. They live in dark caves, under standing stones, or underground, and are especially numerous on the Pilatus Berg.

It was the day before the cows were to be led down from the mountains. The herdsman had spent the whole day rounding them up. He fell asleep exhausted, without saying his prayers. The next morning, seven cows were missing. After searching for them in vain, the cowherd decided to act as if they were still there. That night he milked and fed his invisible cows. He left the high meadow and led his cows to the valley, caring for both the visible and invisible ones throughout the winter. In May, he made a show of leading them once again to the mountains. At milking time that night, his lost cows came home: seven milk-cows and seven healthy calves, herded by a tiny dwarf.

In a small town near Zürich, the Erdmännchen used to come down from the mountain and visit the houses in the valley. They were good friends of the children, bringing them gifts of money, food or toys. One day a dwarf came to one of the children and told him, 'Close your eyes and hold out your hand!'

The boy gladly did so, expecting some gaudy plaything. He was shocked when he opened his hand and saw a piece of black coal lying there. 'I don't want this filthy thing!' he cried and threw it on the floor.

Next morning when the boy awoke, he saw something glittering on the rug and stooped to pick it up. Overnight his piece of coal had turned into a costly jewel!

A poor serving girl once lost her way in the forest. After walking many hours without meeting a soul, she was overjoyed to discover a tiny cottage nestled among the trees. Her knock was answered by seven dwarfs, all brothers. They offered her a meal and a place to stay for the night on condition that she chose one of them as a bed-mate.

The girl agreed, ate heartily and bedded down with the eldest dwarf.

Their sleep was interrupted by a woman from the neighbouring village who had come to speak with the dwarfs on a business matter. But her manner changed suddenly when she caught sight of the dishevelled girl.

'You whore! You're a disgrace to our kind! To do business with these . . . these . . . monsters is one thing, but to sleep with them. . . !'

The girl's protestations that death from cold and hunger seemed worse than the embraces of a dwarf fell on deaf ears. Later that night, the enraged woman returned with two men from the village. They dragged the sleeping dwarfs from their beds, murdered them savagely and set fire to the cottage.

The girl was allowed to escape, barefoot and without a coat, but the shock of her experience remained with her for the rest of her life.

It was common knowledge that the richest man in town was an incorrigible miser, but a poor sick relative decided nonetheless to ask him for help. The woman was so weak that she couldn't manage to walk herself and had to send her daughter. Neither the beauty, nor the youth, nor the obvious poverty of the girl made any impression on the scoundrel. He threw her out of his house in the middle of a terrible storm. Tired from the long walk and from lack of food, she started crying. A young man saw her and took pity on her. He had only one cheese left but gave it to her without hesitation. 'Take this, you need it more than I do,' he said with a reassuring smile.

Even his kindness didn't change the girl's luck. She had only gone a few steps when the cheese slipped from her hands and rolled into a ravine.

'Now I have nothing to bring to my mother!' She started to cry again.

Just then, a voice beside her said, 'I found your cheese at the bottom of the ravine, and have brought it back to you. I've also brought some tea for your mother. Give her some as soon as you get home, and she will recover.'

The girl thanked the Herdmanndli profusely and hurried home, before she had time to lose the second gift.

The herb tea quickly restored her mother's health and the cheese turned into pure gold. That night a storm loosed an avalanche, burying the miser's house. The girl and her mother lived in peace and comfort on the money from the golden cheese.

Poor people called them the big-eared dwarfs, and had good reason to like them. They not only brought luck to the whole valley but also stole flour from the greedy miller to make cakes for themselves and for the hungry. Only the miller disliked them. In fact, he hated them and always tried to think of new ways to discourage them. He poisoned a sack of flour and left it where the dwarfs would be likely to find it. But the Erdmännchen were too smart to eat the poisoned flour, and the miller came to regret his action.

From that day on he had no luck and, bit by bit, lost all his lands and possessions. When he had only one sack of flour left, he decided to apologize to the Erdmännchen and make them a gift of it. It was too late. On his way to the dwarfs' burrow, they met him and tumbled him off a cliff.

RED CAPS

SOME of the most bloodthirsty Scottish elves are the Lowland castle spirits. They are called *Red Caps*, Redcombs, Bloody Caps, Dunters or Powries, and by some accounts are said to live only in castles with a history of violence. Others say they live in all Lowland peel-towers.[1] It may well be that both accounts are true, judging by the bloody nature of Scottish history. The Red Caps' main occupation is colouring their red caps, which they dye with human blood. They throw boulders on to travellers from their towers, then catch the blood in their caps. As soon as the blood dries and the colour fades, the Red Caps look for new victims. They also foretell disasters by making a loud noise like the beating of flax. The only things that discourage them are crosses, cross-handled swords and words from the Bible.

Identification: The Red Caps are short, old elves with a sturdy build, long grey hair and red hats. They are about four feet tall, have long protruding teeth, fiery red eyes and eagle-taloned fingers, and wear heavy boots and carry a staff.

Habitat: They live in Scottish towers.

[1] Fortified houses or towers.

A Red Cap

ƜICHƮLN

IN SOUTHERN GERMANY and Austria, the word *Wichtln* refers specifically to house sprites. Like the word 'fairy', it has been so often misused that it is very hard to separate the 'real' Wichtln from those who only carry the name.

One of the most unusual characteristics of the Wichtln is their tireless energy. They will not stop until all their work is done. When they are in a mischievous mood, they will continue their games until their victims are maddened with anger and frustration.

Their tricks are countless. They pull the covers off sleepers, tickle them with ice-cold hands, paint snouts on their faces and glue cow tails to their backs, make the servants spill the milk, tug at girls' braids, mix the mustard and sugar in the pantry, jump on people's backs, tie the cows together and tangle their tails, let the pigs loose, hide the children in the chicken coop, steal the jam, throw hay around, make church-goers fall into puddles, and board up the front door during the night.

When the Wichtln are not busy playing, they do most of the house and farm work, caring for the children, feeding the animals, cleaning up, baking, fetching water and protecting the house from danger. Like most elves, they do not like to be paid for their work with clothing, and will leave if openly presented with a suit or jacket. In some cases, however, they do accept gifts if left quietly in their favourite spots.

Identification: Wights is a generic name in England for elves; Vaettir the generic name in Iceland and Norway. A subspecies of Faroe Island elves is called Vattar, but the most specific use of the name is the southern German Wichtln. It applies to a species of house elves less than three feet tall with hairy bodies, long silver beards, large heads, deep-set eyes, big bellies, spindly legs and deep voices like goitrous men. They dress in old-fashioned peasant clothes or in red jackets with red stockings, and frequently carry a birch walking-stick.

The Füttermännchen, who specialize in feeding farm animals, the Pechmanderln, who glue sleepy children's eyes shut with pitch, and the extremely mischievous Pitzln are all subspecies of Wichtln.

Wichtln are often confused with other species. Butzen or Putzen are sometimes improperly called Wichtln though they should be classed as ghosts or revenants. Käsermänner are also called Wichtln, although they are usually large, more giants than elves; they live in the mountain huts where cheese is made.

Habitat: Austrian, Swiss and south German Wichtln live in woods, in houses, in high summer meadows, in caves and in barns. Unlike the NORGGEN, they are not wood spirits but domesticated earth spirits.

A ferryman on the Werra was once approached by two small men who asked him to take them across the river. As he neared the middle with his passengers, he was surprised to find that his boat was floating very low in the water. He only succeeded in reaching the other bank with great difficulty.

'What would you prefer as payment,' his two passengers asked him, 'a sack of salt, or a piece of gold for each passenger?'

The ferryman reckoned that the salt would be of more use to him than two pieces of gold. He told them he would take the salt.

'You should have chosen the gold,' they replied. 'Turn around and look over your right shoulder. You will see just how many passengers you had.'

The man did as he was told and suddenly saw the whole

A Wichtl

plain swarming with little men, hundreds and thousands of them.

Saddened by his bad luck, the ferryman poled slowly back across the river. It was only some weeks later that he discovered that he had not made such a bad choice after all: his sack of salt was still as full as the day he got it, and remained that way until his death.

A Wichtl once fell in love with a beautiful girl. He courted her night and day, begging her to take him for her lover. But the girl turned him down flat, laughing at his pleas.

'How can a tiny old man like you hope to win me for your bride? Why, you're old enough to be my father, and ugly to boot!'

For a long time, blinded by his love, the Wichtl put up with the girl's rudeness. But finally he could stand it no longer. When he saw her flirting with and caressing a good-looking young man, he lost control.

He waited until the girl was alone in a hut high in the mountains and then started an avalanche on the adjoining slope. Within a few minutes, the hut was gone, buried under tons of snow.

Only then did the Wichtl realize what he had done. Frantically, he dug in the snow for the body of his sweetheart. He dragged her to the nearest crucifix and laid her gently under the cross, sobbing for his lost love.

church
GRIMS

MANY churches in Scandinavia and England are haunted by elves. Despite the Dark Elves' normal aversion to churches and church bells, these elves seem to have no fear and even go so far as to make their homes in the bell towers or under the altars. They take little interest in church activities but are able to foretell the death of any parishioner.

The Swedish Kyrkogrims are said to derive from souls of animals sacrificed by early Christians at the building of each new church. Although the practice of animal sacrifice has long since died out, the Kyrkogrims have not. Even present-day churches have their attendant spirits. Finnish Kirkonwäki live in groups, only asking for human help when one of their women is in childbirth. The English *Church Grim* is similar to the Kyrkogrim, except for his impulsive and mischievous delight in ringing church bells loudly at midnight.

Identification: Church Grims are usually less than two feet high, misshapen and dark-skinned.

Habitat: Although church elves are most common in northern Europe, church-living spirits have been reported in Greece. However, there is some doubt as to their origins, and as to whether they should be more correctly classed as monsters or as elves.

The northern sprites can be found in Denmark, Sweden, Finland and Yorkshire. The Yorkshire Church Grims like to live in bell-towers, the Finnish Kirkonwäki under the altar and the Danish Kirkegrims in dark places in the main nave of the church.

Quiet Folk

THE *Quiet Folk* are not as boisterous as their ERDLUITLE relatives but are a gentle and peaceable tribe if left undisturbed. Because they have lived for so many thousands of years in the depths of the earth, they know the hiding places of all ores and precious stones, and are extremely wealthy. Any human foolish enough to attempt to cheat them of their gold will only succeed in angering them.

The Quiet Folk give gifts of staggering generosity to their favourites or those who have served as judge in one of their many arguments, helped a female dwarf in childbirth, or provided a hall for their wedding feasts.

The wealth of the Quiet Folk is not limited to jewels and gold. They know the healing properties of all plants and stones and are so skilful in their application that they are never sick. They also have great power over all 'magical' everyday activities such as bread-baking, beer-brewing, spinning and weaving, and are undisputed master-smiths. A man who has offended the Quiet Folk can never hope to be a good blacksmith, and the house in which he lives will be plagued with bad beer, moth-eaten clothes and mouldy bread.

The peaceful, introverted nature of the Quiet Folk sometimes verges on sullenness and bad temper. They have been known to throw temper-tantrums upon hearing the sounds of church bells, drums or farm machinery, and become violent if the Church is even mentioned. Among the Quiet Folk's other hatreds are humans who treat them badly, break promises, are by turns friendly and unfriendly, or, worst of all, force the Quiet Folk to show their goose feet. Angry Quiet Folk should be avoided at all costs. They are slow to anger, but when angry are impossible to calm. In fits of choler, they have been known to lame children, carry away women, sicken men and make adults lose their reason.

Identification: Local names for the Quiet Folk or Stille Volk, as they are called in Germany, are many and varied. The Lithuanians call them the Karlá, the Danes the Unners-Boes-Töi or Untüeg, the people of the Harz Querxe, and yet others Kepetz, Böhlers-Männchen, Malienitza, Zinselmännchen, Krosnyata, Kaukas and Onnerbänkissen. Similar dwarfs in Wales are called Gwarchells, in northern England Yarthkins.

The adult dwarfs are between one and a half and two and a half feet high and wear coarse black clothing and red or grey hats which give them the power of invisibility as well as extraordinary strength and courage. Their skin is black, their arms long, their eyebrows and beards thick and bushy. Their bodies are often crooked and misshapen, and their feet like those of ducks or geese. They can live to be two thousand years old, although full-grown at the age of three. Their hair turns grey a little before their fourth birthday.

Habitat: The ERDLUITLE are southern Germany's dwarf family, the Quiet Folk the northern branch. They have settled thickly in Denmark, along the Baltic coast, in northern and eastern Germany and can be found in parts of England, Holland, Poland, Czechoslovakia and Romania. Strictly subterranean elves, they strongly dislike sunlight, and will go to great lengths to avoid it, only appearing at night. They make their homes under houses, barns and hill mounds, and occasionally in caves. They refuse to live beneath horse or cow stalls because of the filth that drips into their houses.

'Please take me with you! I won't cause any trouble!'
'We'll let you come, but only on two conditions. You must

not speak and under no circumstances may you take anything away with you. Put on this cap,' the leader said, handing the man an old battered hat, 'and follow us. Tonight we're going to a wedding, so you'll find plenty of food and drink.'

The man did as he was told and in a few seconds found himself in a large banquet hall. At first terrified that one of the guests would see him, he soon lost his fear. The cap made him completely invisible! His dwarf companions, protected by their caps-of-darkness, were not at all shy: one stood at the shoulder of each guest, eating the food from his plate and stealing the wine from his cup.

'That's not a bad idea!' thought the young man, and began to stuff food into his mouth as fast as he could. After thoroughly enjoying himself, he thought of his wife and children. He felt guilty, for they often had to go hungry.

'No one will notice just *one* piece of bread, and my wife would certainly appreciate it. One piece won't hurt anyone,' he thought and slipped some bread into his pocket.

But someone did notice. In a second, the dwarfs had vanished from the hall, leaving their friend behind and, what's more, taking his cap with them. The poor man was now visible to the wedding guests. He had a lot of explaining to do and a long walk ahead of him. You see, he lived a hundred miles away.

I t was a hot day and the work was hard. The two boys ploughing their father's land wished there was some way to escape, a nice cool stream to bathe in, some girls to tease or something to eat. Soon all they could think of was food – home-baked bread, a cool drink to wash it down with. And then they began to *smell* it. Freshly brewed beer and the odour of newly baked bread.

'If only we could have some of that beer! And some of that bread!' the boys chorused.

One of the Quiet Folk

The smell continued to tantalize them as they trudged to the end of the furrow. Suddenly, it grew stronger. Lying on the ground before them were two mugs of beer and a loaf of warm bread.

The boys ate and drank with great relish. 'Thank you!' the second boy called out and threw a few coins into his empty cup.

'You fool!' the other said. 'Those dwarfs don't know the difference between coins and dirt. You can throw *your* money away, but I'm going to give them dirt!'

Before the end of the year, that boy was dead, while his friend lived in health and peace.

A poor woman of Geislingen was asked to serve as midwife for a she-dwarf. Instead of her customary payment, the woman was given an apronful of coal by the tiny father. Although upset by the poverty of the gift, the midwife didn't have the courage to scold the little man. She started back home with her husband.

About halfway there, the woman began to feel the weight of the coal in her apron and wanted to throw it away. As the first pieces of coal hit the ground, she heard a voice behind her. 'The more you throw away now, the more you'll have to beg later on!'

Turning around, the woman saw a little man dressed in leather.

'Who do you think you are? I can throw a few worthless pieces of coal away if I feel like it,' she yelled, but by then the dwarf was gone.

'I don't think you should have talked to him like that,' her husband said. 'You never know with the Little People. Maybe there is some truth in what he said. Keep the coal until we get home. Then we can see if there is anything to his story.'

With a certain amount of bad grace, the midwife did as her husband said, and was fully rewarded when she got home. The remaining lumps of coal had turned into precious gold coins.

It was 1883, and the moon was full. Its cruel harsh light shone down on the countryside, reflecting and refracting against the particles of frost in the air. The full moon always inspires a certain awe, but this was a full moon over the Transylvanian landscape. Maybe out of fear of their own stories of werewolves and monsters, and maybe out of the realization that these creatures were not entirely imaginary, the townspeople stayed safely indoors that night.

A widow sat in her kitchen watching the leaves fall from the trees and thinking of the stories her father had told her. Was it true that the forest had come right up to the house and that strange creatures had knocked on the door? With a shiver, she turned toward the stove. There, sitting on it, was one of the Old Ones! He wore a red old-fashioned jacket and a black cap. His arms, chest and face were hairy and his feet were webbed like a duck's. The woman was too scared to move. The little man warmed himself happily by the fire and chattered in the moonlight.

After her visitor had left, the woman could not sleep. Were the Old Ones really coming back? Would they take her house away from her? This one had been no bigger than her arm but had acted as if he were lord and master. What should she do if he came back?

Tired out by too much speculation, the woman fell asleep as dawn lightened the room.

After waiting all day for her visitor to reappear, she was almost disappointed when he came that night. 'Out, you monster, and let a God-fearing woman sleep!' she cried.

Before she could defend herself, the little man leaped from the stove and scratched her forehead. For the next three days, the woman struggled between life and death, sick with fright and fever.

One can't be sure whether this was an isolated experience or whether the full moon encouraged other Old Ones that night. In any case, the woman was never bothered again by nightly visitors.

A farmer took extraordinary pride in his beer. The others had to agree that it was the best in the parish, but still thought he was a little too vain. You can imagine their delight when they discovered that the beer was disappearing from his cellar! Try what he would, the farmer couldn't catch the thief or stop the theft.

This state of affairs continued for several weeks, and the jealous neighbours thought that God must certainly be punishing the man's vanity. Then one day the farmer was on his way through the forest when a voice called out from among the trees, 'Pingel is dead! Pingel died! Pingel is dead!' The farmer thought this unusual enough to tell his wife when he returned home. It is not every day that one hears voices in the forest, and he had never heard of anyone by the name of Pingel and couldn't imagine why his death could be so important.

But the dwarf who had been stealing the farmer's beer knew why. He cried out from the cellar, jug in hand, 'Oh, no! Pingel's dead! Pingel's dead! Then I've taken beer enough from here. Oh, Pingel's dead! Pingel's dead!'

In his grief, the dwarf let the jug fall. He ran off into the woods to search for the body of his sick friend, Pingel, whom he had hoped to cure with the farmer's tasty brew. From then on, the beer was safe in the cellar and the neighbours had to learn to live with their jealousy.

Quiet folk changelings

THE least understood QUIET FOLK are the *Changelings*.

Changelings, or more specifically Kielkröpfe, are left by the QUIET FOLK in place of women or children. Characterized by an outrageous appetite, a foul bad temper and fits of squalling and howling, the Changelings are unwelcome guests in any home. Some consider them the children of the QUIET FOLK, but on closer consideration, they are probably dwarfs too old to work. Forced to change places with robust humans, these old dwarfs must end their days among men. They can only be repatriated if tricked into revealing their age or if they are so badly mistreated that the QUIET FOLK must rescue them. Sometimes misbegotten elf children are exchanged for humans, but never healthy elf babies.

The most civilized method of getting rid of Changelings is to make them reveal their age. One should place a large goose egg in front of them or pretend to brew beer or cook a meal in a small eggshell. This will so fascinate them that in the end they will cry out, 'I'm so old! I'm so old! But I've never seen anything like that!'

Identification: The Quiet Folk Changelings have wrinkled skin and swollen heads. They are incredibly ugly and have bright eyes. The QUIET FOLK make the most extensive use of Changelings, but the practice is not limited to this tribe of elves. Many other European species substitute for humans elves who are unable to work. All these substituted elves are called Changelings.

Habitat: The Quiet Folk Changelings can be found in Germany, Holland, Poland, Czechoslovakia, Romania and parts of England. Other Changelings appear in all European countries.

While spinning was still a common occupation, young people used to gather together a few times a month. They would sing, talk and dance to make the tedious work go faster. All the servants of a castle were at one of these get-togethers. There was much noise and loud talk. Then someone noticed that a bright light was burning in the cellar.

'But there's nobody down there!' squealed a chambermaid in terror.

'Who could have left the light on?' another asked. 'It's so bright!'

'I'm certainly not going down there!' one of the grooms stated. 'You never know, it might be something *heathen*!'

'You're scared of meeting something heathen!' the nurse-maid scoffed. 'And what do you think I have to put up with every day? If that CREATURE I have to take care of is Christian, then I'll leave the Church!'

'Shh. . . . Don't talk that way – you know the priest wouldn't like it.'

'I'll worry about what the priest likes or doesn't like when I don't have to take care of that screaming brat any more. A few months ago, I could sleep at night, eat with my friends, and even have some time to myself. But now! The creature howls all the time, and eats enough for ten grown men. Even bringing its food up the stairs is a full-time job. First it's too cold, then it tears its clothes off and howls some more, and then the mistress is there, blaming me for what's happened to the monster. And you think I'm scared of the light in the cellar? After the life I've been living, a light in the cellar is a relief. I'll go down there and see what it's all about.'

A Quiet Folk Changeling

'Please don't go – something might happen!'

'If something happens, then someone else will have to take care of the creature.' The nursemaid started down the stairs. At first all was quiet, then a voice came from behind the wine casks.

'Since you're peeping, I'm throwing!'

The girl wasn't frightened. 'If you're throwing, I'm catching!' she replied, and held out her apron.

A little to her surprise, something did come sailing through the air: it was the child she was supposed to be caring for, who had been replaced by the creature – the cantankerous changeling. After a little comforting, the baby settled down to sleep. The nursemaid never again saw anything of the changeling upstairs, or its friends in the cellar.

A Danish family was once plagued by a changeling. It had come because their baby hadn't been baptized early enough. The neighbours used to spy on it as soon as the owners left the house. The changeling would then race around, run up the walls like a cat, perch on the rafters, make a racket and howl to itself in some strange language. But if anyone entered the room, he would find the changeling fast asleep, curled up at the end of the table.

At first, nothing could convince the family that the changeling was not their child. Then they noticed its tremendous appetite. The little thing packed away enough food for four men. Between this unwelcome financial burden and the superstitious mutterings of the neighbours, the family soon grew tired of their guest. The serving girl in particular was irked at having to peel fifty potatoes for every meal and having to cook three cabbages instead of one. One day she hit on a plan. She killed a small pig and, without cleaning it in any way, baked it into a large pudding. When she set it in front of the changeling, the creature was delighted. Then it found the hair and hide of the pig inside the pudding.

'What is this?' it asked. 'A pudding with hide? A pudding with hair? A pudding with eyes! And a pudding with legs in it! Well, three times have I seen a young wood by Tiis Lake, and never yet did I see such a pudding! The Devil himself can stay here now!'

That evening, the family was able to enjoy dinner with their own child and was never bothered by a changeling again.

KORRED

STANDING stones or dolmens are a familiar sight in Europe. In Cornwall, Brittany and Iberia, they are an accepted part of the landscape. Often the stones are hidden deep in the woods, half-covered with vegetation, but in other places they are grouped in circles, reminders of ancient civilizations. The Bretons say the dolmens were brought to Brittany by the *Korred*, who were so strong that they were able to carry the massive stones on their backs.

Dolmens were used by the Celts as astronomical markers as well as meeting points and places of worship. But the Celts died out and only the Korred remain to tell the story of the stones. The locals still honour these Old Ones who first brought the stones into the land and who now live in caves underneath them.

The dolmen elves are most common in Brittany, where they appear under myriad different names, but can also be seen in the Pyrenees and in Cornwall. The Breton dwarfs are grouped under the name of Korrs or Korred, and have bright red eyes as well as the Dark Elves' traditional dark skin. In keeping with their association with the standing stones, they are prophets as well as magicians, and know the secrets of all treasures hidden in their neighbourhood. Their main delight is in dancing, which they do with such vigour that the grass burns in circles under their feet. They only dance at night, usually on Wednesday, their holiday. Humans should take care never to join these dances, for they are Korred dances, serious elf rituals which have little to do with our frivolous foot-stompers. The Korred react with violence against humans who disturb these rituals. Girls who take part will bear a child nine months later resembling someone in the village they have never slept with. Men will be forced to dance until they die of exhaustion. The Crions – a kind of Korred – invariably find this so funny that they laugh until daybreak.

The Korred are not always unkind in their dealings with men, although never over-friendly. For a small payment, they loan their oxen, kitchen utensils and tools, and sharpen knives and scythes if these are left overnight on their 'borrowing stones'. Some of the Korred even care for the pigs if they are allowed to watch the smoking and are given a little piece of fat.

The Cornish standing-stone elves are called Spriggans. They guard underground treasures and are responsible for controlling the winds. They resemble the French Crions, but also appear as giants, stretching to enormous size in order to scare humans.

Identification: The original Korred and Crions range from one to three feet in height. The Jetins and Vihans are occasionally even smaller. The Korred's bodies are hunched, their skin black, their hair dark and shaggy, and their eyes, set far back into their heads, are the colour of burned rubies. Instead of fingers, the Korred have cats' claws, as well as goats' hooves in the place of feet. Their voices are cracked and muffled but they have an extraordinarily loud laugh. The male Korred always carry a large leather purse, filled with hair and a pair of scissors. They live together with their wives but the females are rarely seen outside the house.

When the Phoenician sailors came to Brittany, they brought another type of elf with them whom they called Courètes or

A Korred

Carikines. Through the years, these have intermarried with the old Korred until they have been assimilated, and one can barely distinguish between the 'old' Korred and the 'new'. Among the many old Korred still extant are the Jetins, the Hommes Cornus, the Corics, Kerions, Kouricans, Gwazig-Gan, Kourils and Korandon. In one aspect only do the younger Korred differ from the older: most of them do not wear their hair loose but hide it under enormous wide-brimmed hats. Among the many present-day Korred are the Corriquets, Guerrionets, Korriks, Boudiguets, C' Horriquets and Corrandonnets, and the Kornikaned who carry small horns attached to their belts.

Habitat: The Korred live in Brittany, although one entirely male group, the Hommes Cornus, live in Gascony. Other Korred have been occasionally seen in the Pyrenees. The Spriggans emigrated from Brittany to England, and now live exclusively in Cornwall.

The original Korred lived underground, in caves under dolmens, under heaths, in sea-cliff caves or in natural caverns. Their homes had and still have one characteristic in common: they always lie below sea level. The Teuz and Poulpikans, also of old ancestry, make their homes in bogs, swamps, and stagnant waters.

The younger Korred are not as particular about where they make their homes as the older tribes are. They have been spotted near dolmens, at the seashore, among sand dunes and in some extreme cases, even in human habitations.

A hunchbacked farmer and his wife were in the fields one day when some Korred bent on kidnapping them approached. The couple was only saved by some iron in the fork of their plough.

'Let him go, let him go, fork of the plough has he!' sang

the Korred, powerless against the iron's magic.

One night the man went to the Korred, protected by the iron. He joined their dance, after first making them promise not to tire him to death. The Korred's dancing music consisted of the simple song 'Monday, Tuesday, Wednesday!' which the hunchback then completed with 'Thursday, Friday, Saturday'. Grateful, the Korred rewarded the man with a younger face and removed his hump.

Another hunchback from the same village heard of his good fortune and decided to try his luck. He, too, went dancing with the Korred, but stuttered while trying to finish the rhyme. His song sounded something like 'And Su-Sunday too, and Su-Sunday too!' This hardly pleased the Korred. They gave him the hump they had taken from his neighbour and sent him away. Furious, the double-hunchback hurried back to the village.

'Look what happened to me, just because of those Korred. It's your fault, you e-elf-loving swindler! If I hadn't listened to you, I wouldn't have th-th-this *thing* on my back right now! Pay me, or I'll tell everyone in t-town that you're in league with those foul-mouthed d-d-de-devil dwarfs.'

'Here's some money,' said the farmer. 'Now leave me alone.'

The farmer then went to the Korred to finish their rhyme for good: 'With Sunday, as is meet, and so the week's complete.' Now knowing the days of the week, the Korred were able to stop dancing. They presented the farmer with one of their purses filled with horse-hairs, leaves and sand, which changed to gold and precious jewels when sprinkled with holy water.

A Cornish woman lost her child to the Spriggans. They left a changeling which gave her no end of trouble. Caring for the ugly creature took up most of the poor woman's day, and thinking of ways to get rid of it most of the night.

A friend told her that she could only free herself of the monster by dipping it in a holy well. The young mother took her friend's advice. She travelled to the well and dipped the changeling twice into the cold water. As she was about to duck it the third time, she heard voices coming from inside the well. The voices were so loud and so strange that she forgot her task and ran back to the house, too frightened to look behind her.

Once she was safe at home, the woman's fear turned to anger. She decided to rid herself of the changeling, once and for all. She took a broom from the cupboard, set the changeling on the rubbish heap and beat it, paying no attention to the creature's cries. She then stripped it naked and left it beside the church stile.

When the woman awoke in the morning, her own child was back in its cradle, and the changeling had vanished, never to be seen again.

DUSKY
ELVES

Fées

THE word 'fée', like 'fairy', has been constantly misused. Although the *Fées* were originally nature and fertility spirits of great age and power, the name has come to mean gentle fairy godmothers who always travel with a blue ball dress and a magic wand. In folk belief they are still held to be some of the oldest beings on this planet, born long before the mountains or seas were formed, in the very beginning of time.

The Fées dispersed and looked on as the hills, trees, plants, animals and men took shape. The Fées who found themselves in the woods became wood ladies, caring for the trees, flowers and wild animals. The Fées of the plains carried dolmens into the land, holding them on top of their heads or balancing them on their spindles. The field Fées grew long breasts and threw them over their shoulders, suckling the children on their backs and bringing fertility to the land. The mountain Fées controlled the avalanches and nurtured the delicate spring wild flowers. The Fées who lived underground gathered together all the buried treasures and stood watch over them, unearthing them when they thought it necessary. The fog Fées travelled on the wind, shrouding the streams and rivers with thick white clouds that refreshed the earth and frightened trespassers.

Then, in the nineteenth century, the Fées disappeared. Their absence was strongly felt in Brittany where the peasants said their departure was due to the advent of the 'invisible' century and that they would return in the 'visible' century, the twentieth. To date, there has been no documentation of returning Fées, although if they did return they would gather in secret, out-of-the-way places, far from the curious eyes of humans and the disturbances of civilization, electricity and cars.

Since most men know very little about Fées and have never seen one, it is important, if the Fées do return, that one should know how to deal with them. Like all elves, the Fées should be treated with respect and never insulted or mocked. They should not be stopped from borrowing things from house or farm but made welcome to what they need. Whatever they use, they always return and, if it is damaged, always repair it. Beyond that, the Fées bring luck to any house they visit.

At daybreak, no attempt should be made to keep them away from their homes. When they give advice, it should be followed to the letter, no matter how far-fetched or preposterous it may sound. The Fées' gifts should only be used as directed and under no circumstances should other humans be told of such presents. Women who are called by the Fées to serve as mid-wives should go with good cheer and do their work well, and they will be richly rewarded. Men and women should be careful not to get locked into a stare with the Fées, for the Fées always win; sometimes the Fées' eyes are so hypnotic that the human is drawn into an abyss. No human should disturb the Fées' wash: its proverbial whiteness is their joy. Men should be warned not to enter into too intimate relation-ships with the Fées. Their concepts of love-making are more extreme than those of humans. It is even dangerous to dance with the Fées. Their dances, wild whirlwinds of song and movement, last the whole night through and are so tiring that men who take part in them die of exhaustion.

Identification: Because of their various residences, the Fées differ widely in shape and form. Most of them are between two and four feet high and can take the shapes of humans, moles, bats or small animals. The Fées are beautiful, their beauty marred by one animal flaw such as duck feet, a snake's tail, or hairy bodies. Females predominate over males, and dress in white with long blonde hair; they are gifted with long life and have the power of invisibility.

Among the almost infinite number of subspecies are the Martes, dark hairy women with fiery eyes and long breasts that reach to their knees; the Sœurettes, who act like the Bacchantes of ancient Greece; the Sauvageons, who are of incredible age; the Fayettes, who love to change into moles; the Demoiselles Blanches, blonde women dressed in white who live in the fog; the male Féetauds; the Hades; Blanquettes; Margot-la-Fée; the Fayules; the tiny Fäies; the Spanish Hadas, the Swiss Fadhas; and the mountain Fée des Vertiges, who appears as a flame-like abstraction.

Habitat: The Fées live in almost every conceivable corner of nature. They have been seen in trees, on mountains, near rivers, in lakes, beside waterfalls, in caves and on bridges. Some live next to the KORRED underneath dolmens. Most live in crystal caves underground, while others prefer natural caves in the mountains or by the sea. They are widespread throughout France, the Alps, the Pyrenees and the islands off the French coast. The Spanish and Portuguese Hadas and Fadas are so similar to the French Fées that their origins are probably the same.

Two fishermen of the Haute-Bretagne once had the luck to see two Fées transforming themselves into humans. The elves smeared their eyes with a special grease which they kept in a small jar. Suddenly there they were, two townswomen, as human as humans, and not to be told from them in any way!

A Corsican once caught a beautiful Fée and made her his wife. The only conditions the lake woman imposed on her husband were that he never remind her of her ancestry or comment on her eating and drinking habits.

All went well between the two for twenty years and they had six children, three boys and three girls. The man was true to his promise and never said anything about his wife's origins. The only thing that bothered him about their marriage was that his wife never ate at the table, but always took the leftovers into her room and brought the plates out empty.

The man grew more and more curious as to what his wife was doing with the leftovers, and how she managed to stay alive on so little food. Then he spied on her through the keyhole. What he saw put a quick end to his curiosity and an even quicker end to his marriage. His wife, instead of eating the food, poured it into a hole in her back.

'You inhuman wretch,' the man called out to her, 'now I know your horrible secret, and I don't want to have any part of it. Pack your bags and leave this house. I thought I had married a Fée and not some alien monster!'

The woman did not wait to be told twice. A few minutes later, she left with her three daughters and went back to her old life. Before she left, she put a curse on the family, decreeing that there would never be more than three male heirs alive at once for the next seven generations.

The inhabitants of a small Swiss town never had to rely on prophets or almanacs to foretell the weather for the coming year. Each winter, a Fée came out of the mountains, herding a flock of white goats in plentiful years, and black goats in years of famine, war or plague.

Ꝺomovɪᴙᴇ

THE *Domoviye* are among the most important Slavic house
elves, although their name is sometimes used for other species.
They can make a household run smoothly if they are well
treated, but if dissatisfied will ruin its owners. The Domoviye
(singular Domovoy) do favours for the family, stealing food
and grain from the neighbours, cleaning the house and taking
care of the animals. The Domoviye live behind the stove in
the corner of the house facing the religious and family icons.
Extremely loyal to his home, the Domovoy will often stay on
even after the family has moved away. He foretells the future,
warns of disasters and wakes the owner of the house if there
is a fire or robbery. When someone in the house is close to
death, the Domovoy moans, groans and starts to wail. If the
master of the house must die, the Domovoy cries hunched
over his work, his cap covering his face.

Great care should be taken not to make the Domovoy
jealous. When the autumn offering of a goose is given to the
VODYANY, the head should be kept and hung in the goose shed,
so that the Domovoy will not notice that one of his geese is
gone. If he realizes that one is missing, and that it has been
given to another elf, he will be very angry. One should also
be careful on 30 March. Then the Domovoy always has an
attack of bad temper, most likely because he is changing his
skin. On this day he should be given food, and the cattle and
chickens should be kept indoors.

The Domovoy receives other gifts throughout the year,
one of the most important being an offering of stewed grain
on 28 January. If it is forgotten, there are two ways to remedy
the mistake. A wizard can come and sacrifice a black hen to
the Domovoy, or the master of the house can go at midnight
into the courtyard, face the moon, and call to the Domovoy,

'Master! Stand before me as the leaf before the grass, neither black nor green, but just like me! I have brought you a red egg!'* The Domovoy will calm down as soon as he receives the egg.

When moving into a new house, precautions must be taken to keep strange Domoviye out. A bear's head in the stable will usually scare off intruders. If the family moves to a home within walking distance, the oldest woman in the family should light a fire in the stove of the old house. At noon she should rake the coals into a clean jar and cover them with a white cloth. Opening both house doors, she should call towards the stove, 'Welcome, grandfather, to our new home.' Arriving at the new house, she should strike both door-posts and ask, 'Are the visitors welcome?' The master and mistress of the house must reply, 'Welcome, grandfather, to the new spot!'* and lay out offerings of bread and salt. The old woman is then free to enter the house. Once the fire is transferred to the new stove, the carrying-jar should be broken and buried. The house, blessed with fire and Domovoy, is then ready to be occupied.

Identification: The Domoviye are covered with dark hair from head to foot. Even the palms of their hands are hairy. They are small enough to fit behind the stove and are only seen at night.

In Kirov, the Domovoy is an old man the size of a five-year-old child. He wears a red shirt and a blue girdle, and has a white beard, mousy white hair, red eyes and an old man's face. In East Germany he usually wears white, and in Poland is called Iskrzycki, or 'spark'. All Domoviye grumble, quarrel and swear.

Habitat: The Domoviye are found throughout European Russia, in Poland and in some parts of eastern Germany and Czechoslovakia. They either live behind the stove or, as in the case of the Iskrzycki, inside it.

A Domovoy

On a lonely hill in Poland, the ruins of an old house can still be seen. It is reportedly haunted by a Domovoy. The owners were forced to leave in a hurry and weren't able to take him along. Still loyal, despite their desertion, he has remained in the ruins, rarely moving from the old stove.

A southern Polish house was also said to be haunted because every child who lived there died suddenly and mysteriously. For many years no one would live there. Finally a poor man decided to try it. He gathered his family and their few possessions together and set out for the 'haunted house'.

When they arrived, he opened the door, and said in a loud and friendly voice, 'Good day to whoever lives here!'

The Domovoy, hearing himself addressed so politely, answered the man. 'Good day to *you*. If you want to stay in my house you are welcome, but only on the condition that you have your wife grease and clean the stove every week and don't let the children lie on it.'

Pleased with his good luck, the man thanked the Domovoy and moved in. His wife was very careful to clean the stove and the children were not allowed near it. The couple now had a good house but were unfortunately just as poor as before. One night the husband complained about how little they had to give the children to eat. Just then, he heard a strange sound behind him and turned around to see the Domovoy dragging a large pot of pure gold out of the stove.

'Because you've taken such good care of the house, here is a present for you,' said the Domovoy. 'Now your children won't have to go hungry.'

One day a Domovoy behaved mischievously, knocking things over and finally picking up the house cat and throwing her across the room.

At that point the mistress of the house lost her temper. This time, the Domovoy had gone too far.

'Grandfather!' she shouted at him. 'Shame on you! Don't you know better than to bother the cat? The poor thing has a lot of work to do, keeping the mice out of the pantry and the rats out of the house. I don't want to ever see you bothering her again. You are important, but so is the cat. Too important for you to take your bad temper out on her.'

After this scolding, the Domovoy grumbled a little, but never touched the cat again.

VAZILY BAGANY AND BANNIKI

THE *Bannik* lives inside the bath house, guarding it jealously. It is not wise ever to bathe after dark, because then the Bannik takes his own bath. If disturbed, he will suffocate the intruders. In Smolensk, the locals have such respect for him that they always leave a full bucket of water and a bath whisk for him and his friends.

The *Vazila* is a DOMOVOY who takes care of the horses. He resembles the house DOMOVOY but has horse's ears and hooves.

The *Bagan* is the protector of all farm animals, especially goats and horses. It is advisable to keep him in mind when buying livestock. The animal must be of the right colour or the Bagan will torture and bother the poor beast until it is almost dead. If he approves of the animal's colour, it will grow fat and sleek and never sicken. To discover the Bagan's favourite colour, a piece of cake should be taken at Easter, wrapped in a rag and hung in the stable for six weeks. Then it should be taken out and inspected for maggots. If the maggots are white, then the Bagan's favourite colour is white, if red, then the colour is red.

Identification: The Banniki and Bagany are very similar in appearance to the DOMOVIYE. The Bagan is only visible on Holy Thursday and on Easter Sunday. The Vazily have horse's ears and hooves.

Habitat: The Bagan lives behind the stove or in the barn. The Bannik lives in the 'banya' or bath house, while the Vazila is usually seen in the stable. They inhabit the same areas of eastern Europe as the DOMOVIYE.

'**T**his is the last money we have. Please be careful with it.' The woman handed her husband their savings and sent him off to buy a horse at the market.

In town the man could only find one horse for the money: a tired old nag who looked about ready to drop.

When he arrived home with the new horse, his wife was furious.

'I told you to buy a *horse*, but you bought a worthless lump of dog food. That *thing* won't even live until next week! She'll die like all the rest, and then what will we do?' The woman burst into tears.

Humiliated and embarrassed, her husband led the horse into the barn.

There he got a much better reception. As soon as the barn Domovoy set eyes on the horse, he began to laugh and clap his hands.

'That's really a horse! Finally, a good horse. After all the others, finally a good horse! You're a genius! Now, that's what I call a HORSE!'

The man couldn't believe his ears. What was the Domovoy talking about? Then it dawned on him. The Domovoy only liked one colour, and this nag had it.

Within a week, thanks to the Domovoy's attentions, the worthless mare had turned into a sleek, proud horse. Even the wife was forced to admit that her husband had, indeed, made a good bargain.

fir BOLG

QUEEN MAEVE of the SIDHE is not the only queen in Faerie. Each inland fort or sea-coast rath[1] has its own queen. Her subjects are smaller and less powerful than the tall, stately SIDHE and are often born of human parents. This second group of Faeries are called *Fir Bolg*. They are about three feet in height and wear peasant clothes. They have had enough contact with humans to have earned the name 'good neighbours'. They share the SIDHE's loathing of iron, electricity, new religions and holy water.

Identification: The Fir Bolg are three feet high when on particular errands. (Fir Darig is a two-and-a-half-foot-high man dressed in red who loves to come and sit by the fire.) Like most elves, they are shape-changers and can take on human form. They are stouter and darker than the SIDHE, and some have large pot-bellies. They dress in local peasant costumes of the eighteenth century, preferring red and plaids. They are mortal,

[1] Prehistoric Irish hill-fort.

and are substituted for cows or humans from the upper world when they grow old.

Habitat: The Fir Bolg always live underground, deep inside raths and green hilly mounds. They are Irish natives.

Richard was a real rake. He could be found at every party, dressed to kill, strutting and parading before a bevy of admiring girls. He was the best dancer in the county and never shy of boasting about it. However, his vanity couldn't go unnoticed, and the following Saturday night Richard paid for his thoughtlessness.

'So he says he's the best dancer? Who does he think he is? Even our cripples can dance better than that liar!' A Faery hit Richard squarely in the hip with an arrow and this time he couldn't laugh it off. He had to hobble home accompanied by the silent laughter of the Faeries.

Soon Richard's character began to change. By the end of the week his parents suspected that something was wrong. If he had been hard to handle before, now he was impossible, always whining and moaning, and what's more, eating enough for four hungry bears.

A meeting was called. The neighbours sat in the next room debating and finally decided to put a bagpipe near the bed to see if Richard would play it.

For a few hours, nothing was heard. Then the plotters' patience was rewarded. From Richard's room came the strains of a jig so well executed that even the best piper in town could not have played it. All were now convinced that a changeling had taken Richard's place and talked of how to rid themselves of it.

'One thing the Faeries really hate is the foxglove. If we boil some of the blossoms and then bathe him in the water, he'll be sure to leave.'

One of the Fir Bolg

'By the time you've *picked* the flowers he'll have hidden himself. I say throw him in the mill stream and see what he thinks of *that*!'

'He wouldn't like to be thrown on the fire, either.'

'We have to do something soon. The fire tongs are red-hot. Let's get him!'

They stormed into the room but the bed was empty. Then they saw his face peering through one of the windows. They went after him with the tongs. He howled and vanished into the night, and when they turned around, the real Richard was back. He had learned his lesson and never bragged again.

A woman was walking along the road when suddenly a man appeared before her.

'Would you come and comfort a child that's crying?' he asked. She agreed. He led her through an entrance in the side of a hill to a large room where a baby was crying in its cradle and an old man moaning in the corner. The woman soon stopped the child's tears, but no one could quiet the old man.

'What's wrong with him?' she whispered to the Faery who had brought her inside.

'Come outside with me. See that cow over there? We need the milk for the child. The old man will be put in the cow's place this evening. That's why he's crying.'

That evening the woman passed the hill again on her way home. The cow was dead. All the poor people of the town were gathered around it, trying to snatch a piece of meat. Little did they know that it wouldn't be beef they'd be eating that evening!

The Faeries often steal young women, and those who die in childbirth are taken to Faerie to nurse faerie children. A Galway man had just lost his young wife. He hired a wet nurse to care for the baby, and after a month was surprised to find it so healthy and full of life.

'If you knew what I know, then you wouldn't be so surprised,' said the woman. 'Your wife comes back every night, warms herself by the fire, eats some potatoes and milk, feeds the child, then looks at the bedroom and gives a great sigh.'

The husband decided he would stay up that night to regain his wife. She came, warmed herself by the fire, ate, fed the child and sighed in the direction of the bedroom. But her husband was too scared to move, let alone touch her.

The next day he told her two oldest brothers that she had returned. Night came. When they saw her they, too, were too terrified to catch her.

The next night her youngest brother, the weakling of the family, decided to try *his* luck. He slipped out of bed at the last minute and grabbed her by the arm. She screamed and begged him to let her go, or else 'They' would kill her. She fought and struggled so hard that the boy had to call his brothers for help. The three wrestled with her until she fell to the floor in a faint. Then the youngest brother kept watch over her until the priest came and said a few prayers. The woman was safe from the Faeries but she had a far-away, wild look in her eyes to the day she died.

Ragweed stalks stood half-broken, scattered throughout the yard. In a fit of orderliness, a man cut down most of the untidy stalks, bundled them together and threw them on the fire.

A few days later, a faerie man approached his wife. 'I don't want to seem unneighbourly, but you've been making too much fire.'

The woman was taken aback, for they had only had two fires in the last week.

'When you've too much fire, we've too few horses. Tell your husband to leave the ragweed alone.'

The woman followed the Faery's advice, and never saw her neighbour again.

sleigh beggey and tylwyth teg

THE Manx and Welsh Faeries are of the same elven race as the Irish FIR BOLG, but owing to their geographic isolation and the great passage of time, each group has developed distinct characteristics. The *Sleigh Beggey* or Mooinjer Veggey were the original inhabitants of Man and lived there long before the giants. Since then they have had considerable contact with humans as well as with Irish and Welsh Faeries, but still retain their individuality. The *Tylwyth Teg* peopled Wales somewhat later and intermarried with the already flourishing Ellyllon and GWAGGED ANNWN. Their offspring were the modern lake maidens and the smaller, more mischievous elves known as the Bendith y Maumau.

The entrances to the world of the Tylwyth and the Beggey can be found near their dancing circles, under stones, on open moors, behind caves, under river banks or in ruined castles. A journey to their land almost always involves a passage through water. The doors to it are open once a year, on May Day. It is safest to visit them at that time. Under other conditions, humans taken into their world can only leave after a period of one, five, seven, or a hundred years.

To avoid angering them, special care should be taken to talk about them only in flattering terms, for they can hear anything said outdoors. Consequently, the name Bendith y Maumau means 'mother's blessing' and the Tylwyth Teg are the 'fair family'.

The Tylwyth's one great vice is their delight in stealing blond human children. All possible care should be taken of any fair-skinned babies. They should be baptized at the earliest opportunity and always protected with iron and rowan crosses.

The Sleigh Beggey or 'mob' are also thieves, not of children but of horses. They have their own tiny steeds, but can't resist taking large Irish and English racehorses from the stables. Horses that have been ridden by the Beggey can be recognized by their lathered coats.

The Beggey do not have much contact with human beings and are bound by a large number of ancient taboos which they dare not break. They travel only on certain clearly defined paths. Humans are not allowed to cross their paths when they are in use. The Beggey hate salt, artificial light, horseshoes, silver and all yellow flowers except broom. They are offended by the local custom of strewing ashes near the fireplace on Hallowe'en. The 'crow's feet' seen and studied the next morning by diviners are the footprints of the Beggey. Many Manx families have regretted using this form of divination, for the Beggey always revenge humiliation.

Identification: Both groups are between one and three feet high, quite stocky, shy, and with dark hair and darkish complexions. The Tylwyth Teg and Bendith y Maumau are lighter than the Sleigh Beggey, owing to the Tylwyth's intermarriage with the blonde GWAGGED ANNWN. The Beggey have crow's feet and are occasionally called Feathag.

Habitat: These elves live exclusively on Man and in Wales. Their homes can be revealed with the aid of certain herbs and visited through many entrances here on Earth.

The Tylwyth Teg once took a young boy into their favour. They brought him a few coins every day which he promptly hid. He was very careful never to say a word about the gifts, but then one day his mother discovered the hidden treasure.

'Where did you get *this* from? Tell me, where did you steal it?' the woman cried hysterically. When the boy did not answer, she decided to beat the truth out of him. But still he wouldn't say where he had found the money.

'Please, don't beat me! If I tell you where I got it, I won't get any more. I swear, I didn't steal it!'

His mother didn't believe him and neither did his father. Then the father beat the boy until he gave in.

He told them how the Tylwyth Teg came every day bringing him gifts. But now he had given the secret away, the Tylwyth Teg never set foot in the house again.

In the eighteenth century, farm servants were hired at large hiring fairs twice a year. An elderly midwife and her husband hired a blonde girl named Eilian one Hallowe'en to help with the housework and the spinning. The girl was an excellent worker and spun great quantities of fine flax every night in the meadow in front of the house. She was helped by the Tylwyth Teg, who danced and sang merrily beside her.

By the time spring came, Eilian had vanished. The old midwife told her neighbours that Eilian must have been taken away by her friends the 'fair family'.

Almost a year after Eilian's disappearance her faerie kidnapper came on horseback to ask for the midwife's help. The woman was led to a splendid room in an old fort where a beautiful lady, his wife, lay on a couch. She delivered the baby and was told to rub its eyes with ointment but not to touch her own. Just then, her eye began to itch and, without thinking, she rubbed it. Suddenly she saw that the beautiful lady was really her old serving girl and that the luxurious room was nothing but an empty, cold cave. With the untouched eye, she could still see the fine lady and the beautiful palace. The woman didn't say a word about what had happened, was well rewarded for her work and led safely home.

The next time the midwife went to Caernarvon market, she met and greeted the baby's father.

'With what eye do you see me?' he asked.

She naïvely replied, 'With this one.'

The elf-father picked up a bullrush and thrust it into the woman's 'seeing' eye. She never saw the Tylwyth Teg again, and was half-blind for the rest of her life.

The Tylwyth Teg were once dancing gaily on the moor, hopping over the heather-tops and loudly laughing. Just as their merriment had reached its peak, an old farmer stumbled drunkenly into their midst.

'Well, if it isn't the little ones!' he chuckled and fell with a crash to the ground. In no time at all, he was fast asleep, snoring loudly.

The dancers were outraged. A big oaf like him snoring away in the middle of their dancing-floor! They brought long gossamer ropes out of their hill and tied him hand and foot. Then they covered him with a thin sheet of cobwebbing, hiding him completely from view. Even his snoring couldn't be heard through the cover, and the Tylwyth Teg were able to go on with their dancing.

The old man's family began to worry when he still hadn't returned the next morning. They searched for him everywhere, passing by him several times on the moor.

The following night the Tylwyth Teg took pity on the man, and released him. He wandered for hours without knowing where he was and only regained his sense of direction in the morning, after the first cock had crowed. He then saw that he had been the whole time no more than a quarter of a mile from home.

Norggen
Orculli and
Fänkenmannikins

THE *Norggen* and *Orculli* are small descendants of Orchi, large and malevolent giants who have been known to eat children. The Orculli are of a slightly more pleasant disposition than their Orco relatives. Norggen are usually about three feet high and can be recognized by their blazing red eyes. They can be extremely helpful to humans, telling them when to plant crops, controlling the weather during the harvest season, or helping with the cows. However, when they are in a bad mood, they are as capricious as the Orculli. Their touch alone sickens cows, their breath makes the roads ice over and their ingenuity in leading people astray is nearly boundless. They steal everything: the milk from the milking bucket, the geese from the yard, the laundry from the clothes-line and the stools from under the serving girls. Although they are primarily wood sprites, they are also found inside mines and houses and in the mountains.

The *Fänkenmannikins* are gentle, hairy companions of the large and bloodthirsty Fänggen, or wood giantesses. They are rough-looking and often naked, and haunt the high meadows and mountain dairies. They change leaves into gold, are skilful climbers and live off chamois milk. They often help in dairies, and have control over the weather. The only wind they can't control is the Föhn, a hot, dry xenon-bearing mountain wind. When it begins to blow, the Fänkenmannikins shut themselves up in their caves and won't come out until it has stopped.

The Norggen, Orculli and Fänkenmannikins all have one thing in common: their distrust of shoes. A prankish Orcul can easily be driven away if his victim changes his shoes. The Fänkenmannikins will move away, never to return, if they are presented with some clothing or a pair of shoes.

Identification: The Norggen are between two and three feet high and have red eyes, full beards and strong bodies. They dress in Bavarian loden coats covered with mountain moss, or in old-fashioned green breeches and jackets, with three-cornered hats. They are most often seen between the first moon quarter and the full moon. In some areas, they are called Nörke, Nörkele or Lorggen.

The Fänkenmannikins rarely wear clothes and are hairier and rougher-looking than the Norggen. When it is very cold, they wear simple fur or bark coverings. They are about three feet tall and have a very acute sense of hearing.

The Orculli are master shape-changers and can be recognized by their smell. In northern Italy, one of the worst insults is to say, 'You stink like an Orco!'

Habitat: The Fänkenmannikins live in eastern Switzerland and in the north Tirol. The Norggen are known throughout the eastern Tirol. They originally came from Merano in northern Italy, but have since been found as far north as the German border. The Orculli live in Friuli in northern Italy.

The favourite resting-places of all three elves are valley or mountain caves, although they also visit houses and mines.

The plague had come to Graubünden. Each village counted its dead by the hundreds and the church bells tolled incessantly. Only the wild animals and the wood elves were untouched.

As hysteria rose among the villagers, they decided to find out how the wild men and women stayed so healthy. They went to a stone which was the resting-place of a Fänkenmannikin and filled a hollow in it with wine. They then hid behind some bushes and waited for the Fänkenmannikin to come home. After a while, he came, and was very upset to see his bed filled with red liquid.

'You can't overpower me!' he told the mysterious fluid, and lapped it up down to the last drop. The wine soon took effect, and the Fänkenmannikin grew merry and then merrier.

Just then one of the men jumped out from behind a bush.

'Tell me, little man, what makes you stay so healthy when the plague is killing us like flies?'

The Fänkenmannikin giggled with a hiccup, 'It's pimpernel and silver thistle, but you won't hear *me* tell *you* that!'

The men had the information they had come for. They said goodbye to the Fänkenmannikin, gathered bundles of the two plants and gave them to every person in the village. The plague quickly left Switzerland.

The Nörglein are among the oldest elves. One lived in Eger Field in the Inn River Valley. Each night, he would look up at the nearby Tristkopf Mountain and call out in a loud voice, 'Oh, my God! I'm so old! Think of the Eger Field, nine times a meadow and nine times a forest, and think of the Tristkopf as small as a faun's head! Oh my God, how can I be so old?'

The only answer he ever received was the echo of his own haunting cry.

In the middle of a long, hard winter, a poor peasant woman was asked by a Norgg for shelter. Being kind at heart, she did not hesitate, but led the little man to a warm place by the fire

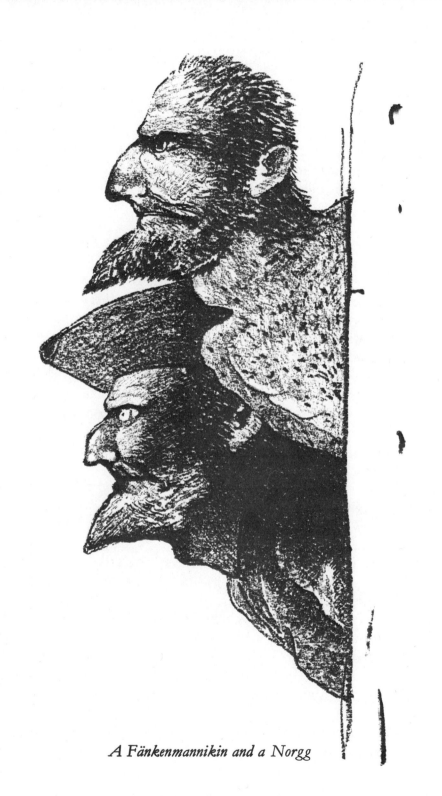

A Fänkenmannikin and a Norgg

and gave him something to eat. He stayed quietly in his corner, accepting the woman's hospitality until January.

The mistress of the house was well rewarded for her kindness. That winter her child never fell out of the cradle, the cow never knocked the milk pail over, none of the potatoes rotted in the cellar and the hens began to lay long before the first thaw.

A rich and powerful count of northern Italy once lost his way in the forest. He was trying to orient himself when he was stopped by a Nörglein and told he was trespassing.

'But I didn't know it was your land. I was out hunting, and lost my way in the woods.'

The Nörglein's red eyes glinted and his beard bristled. 'In *your* territory, you are all-powerful, but this is my land, and here I am the master. The only way you will get out of here alive is to promise me your wife.'

The count argued and protested, but it was no use. Finally, he had to give in to the Nörglein's demands.

He was brought to the fir tree which marked the boundary between their two territories and the Nörglein told him, 'Your wife will have three months to redeem herself. She can try three times to guess my name, and each time she will have three chances. If she does not guess correctly, she will be mine.'

The next two months were sad ones in the count's castle. His wife cried and prayed, while the count sat staring dejectedly at the fire.

Then there were only three days left. The couple set off early in the morning for the wood and came to the fir tree. The Nörglein was already waiting, dressed in clothes of red and green.

'Well, have you thought of a name for me?' he asked.

'Is it Pine? Or Spruce? What about Fir?' the countess asked.

The Nörglein only laughed at her.

The next morning the couple left the castle even earlier than the day before.

'Is your name Oat? Corn? Is it Maize?' she asked.

The Nörglein, this time dressed in blue and red, laughed maliciously.

The next day the couple came so early that there was no sign of the Nörglein. After waiting for a while, the countess saw a path leading off to one side of the fir tree, and decided to follow it. It led to a valley where a tiny house stood, smoke pouring out of its chimney.

'What a darling house!' she exclaimed, and tiptoed up to the window to peek inside.

It was the Nörglein's house. She could see him through the window stirring pots of food on the stove, singing to himself. When the countess heard the words of his song, she could hardly contain herself for joy.

'Oatmeal bubble, cabbage simmer! She'll never guess, the high-born dame, that Purzinigele is my name!'

The countess slipped quietly away from her place at the window and ran back to the fir tree. In a few minutes, the little Norgg came, proudly decked out in his finest clothes of red and gold.

'And, my dear, what is my name today?' he asked, with a wide grin.

'Is it Pur? or Ziege? IS IT PURZINIGELE?'

The Nörglein, livid with rage, stumbled swearing into the underbrush. He was never seen again.

RIVER WOMEN

T HE temperaments of the *River Women* reflect the natures of the waters they haunt. At times, they are as serene as the calmest waters and seek only to delight and charm. A few days later, the waters roar and their mood changes; they drag their victims to the bottom, occasionally even eating them. On the whole, they are not dangerous in the summer and winter but should be avoided in the spring. The German Fenetten should be shunned at all times, for they are so beautiful that any man who sees them must die within the year.

The main occupations of the River Women are singing, hair-combing, dancing and shape-changing. Like all water sprites, they do not like to stay in one form for too long, and appear as humans, fish or fish-women. The French Dracae are especially adept at transforming themselves, and kidnap local women by floating down the river as golden rings, cups or saucers. The poor washer-women cannot resist such treasures and follow them into the water. There they are pulled under by the waiting Dracae, and compelled to serve as nursemaids for the children of their captors.

Identification: The River Women are beautiful, but their beauty is more youthful than that of the MER-WOMEN, and more turbulent than that of the lake maidens, whose peaceful loveliness is a joy to behold. The River Women stand about four feet tall and are very young. Their skin is fair and as soft as velvet; their breasts so long that they are thrown over their shoulders; and their hair is the rich gold colour of river sunsets. The eyes of the River Women are green and they dress in white. They can appear as humans, fish, fish-women, golden baubles or even flowers. When in human form, they can be recognized by the wet tips of their aprons.

Habitat: River Women are common throughout Europe, although they seem to be more prominent in northern Europe. The French and German Fenetten live in the Rhône Valley, the Dracae in southern France, the Nixies in northern Europe and the Kållråden in Sweden. The Greek NEREIDES and the Slavic RUSALKY can be classed as River Women but are not exclusively river elves.

The River Women make their homes in river banks, under tree roots, or in crystal palaces underwater. They come to the surface to comb their hair with gold and ivory combs, seating themselves on lily pads.

The Saal River Nixie was a sensuous and beautiful elf, capable of enchanting even the most unresponsive male. A young farmer once caught a glimpse of her by the riverside. Her image grew and flowered in his mind until she became for him the most desirable creature on earth. He longed to hold her in his arms. Every day he waited for her and was so persistent in his attentions that the Nixie finally let herself be seduced.

The farmer was so thrilled with the Nixie's love-making that he neglected his work to spend more time with her. At first, his wife overlooked his absences, but when he began to stay away for days at a time, her patience came to an end. She followed her husband to the river and found him kissing the lovely water woman.

The wife cried and cursed her husband for his unfaithfulness until his face was red with shame and the Nixie was moved to tears.

'Go,' the River Woman told the farmer. 'You have a wife

and a home. Go back, and never bother me again. If I even find you on the shores of my river, I will kill you.'

As was their custom, the townswomen were down at the stream washing the week's laundry. No weather could keep them from their task. In summer, they laughed as they beat the clothes on the rocks, and in winter the ritual continued, their feet encased in thick boots and their hands red from the cold.

One of the younger women was not hypnotized by the spell of the work. In fact, she was bored. She was cold and the muscles in her arms and shoulders ached from scrubbing. When she was sure she could bear it no longer, she looked up and saw a wooden bowl floating down the stream. She stretched a hand out for it, but it was too far away. She waded further into the water and tried to catch it again, but it was still too far away. Then one of the older women called out to her, 'Be careful, you may be chasing the Drac!' The woman giggled as the girl kept reaching for the bowl.

When the girl finally caught it, she found out that it had in fact been the Drac she was chasing.

Her hand was seized by two strong arms and she was dragged under water.

For seven years, the young woman was not seen again by her washing companions. She lived in the Drac's palace, caring for the women as they gave birth and nursing the children. One day, as she was eating an eel pie, the young woman happened to touch her eye with some of the grease. Suddenly she could see as clearly under water as she had once seen above water. The young woman treasured her new ability, without telling anyone in the palace.

At the end of seven years, she was allowed to return to land. A little later, she met a Drac on her way to market and greeted him cheerfully.

'With what eye do you see me?' the Drac asked her.

'Why, with this one, of course,' she answered, pointing to the eye which she had touched with the grease.

Without hesitating, the Drac put his thumb into it.

'Now you'll never be able to see us again!'

NIXEN AND RIVER MEN

ONE of the most-travelled routes into Elfland will always be through water, fresh water in particular. The *Nixen* and *River Men* are the guardians of this route, welcoming their favourites and blocking the way to the merely curious. They love to seduce young girls and show them the wonders of their underwater homes. Men are guided into their land by the Elf King's Tune, played by the Nixen on golden harps or golden fiddles. Because of their office as the custodians of this route, the Nixen and River Men are particularly dreaded by humans, who fear the 'other' world of the elves as they fear madness, poetry and extreme beauty. From this fear have been fashioned the stories of the 'evil' Necks who suck the souls of their victims, and keep them trapped in cages underwater.

Most accounts, and especially older ones, describe the Nixen and River Men not as bloodthirsty monsters but as water spirits, as moody and alluring as the element in which they live. One day a Nix will appear on the surface of the lake, singing softly and picking sweet melodies on his harp in the sunlight; the next day an angry elf will spew jets of blood from the middle of the lake, raise storms, and demand revenge on those who have wronged him.

Nixen can be helpful towards humans. They warn of drownings, and make the price of grain fall in the markets by buying at high prices. If given the right gifts of black or white goats, hens or roosters, they can be coerced into teaching humans the art of fiddling. But if the Nix teaches a man the Elf King's Tune, the man will not be able to stop fiddling until he plays it backwards, note for note, or until someone cuts the strings of his fiddle from behind.

All humans who want to protect themselves from Nixen and River Men should keep in mind that water elves do not like steel, and can be 'bound' by it into powerlessness. Those who want to be completely safe should also repeat this rhyme before bathing or going near a lake: 'Neck, neck, needle thief, you are in the water, but I am on land. Neck, neck, needle thief, you are on land, but I am in the water.'*

Identification: The northern fresh-water spirits show themselves as handsome young men with curly golden hair and red caps. They are human-sized. The Swedish Strömkarl wears a red cap and cape, as well as red stockings and blue breeches. He loves to sing, and his harping and fiddling are without compare. The Norwegian Fossegrim is similar in appearance, but wears grey clothes. The German Nixen, Seemännlein, Häkelmänner and Nickelmänner and the Scandinavian Söetrolde and Nixen appear as young men with red caps and curly hair, with a golden harp in their hands. They can always be recognized when on land by the wet tips of their shirts or aprons, and by their teeth, which are either green or like those of fish. They can change into fish-men, into horse-men, or into bulls or stallions. The Manx Nikkisen show themselves on full-moon nights, leading the drowned in a long procession.

Habitat: The Strömkarl and the Fossegrim live near water-falls and make their homes in streams or underneath bridges. River Men are known in all northern Europe, from Germany to Finland, as well as in Iceland, England and the Isle of Man.

The wise woman of Ypern was widely known and highly respected because her friendship with a Necker permitted her to ask him questions about the future and the present. A sign hung outside her door read: 'The Necker can answer what anyone asks, be they man or woman.'

A Westphalian man once found a rough-skinned baby lying in the reeds beside a lake. When he picked the boy up, he heard a voice cry out from the middle of the water, 'Don't take my son!' and saw an old man dressed in smith's clothes sitting there, his hands stretched out toward the boy.

The man refused to listen to the voice and dismissed the vision. The boy, nicknamed Roughby because of his strange skin, lived with him for several years and grew to be a fine, strong young man. One day he asked to visit his lake-father. At first the foster-father would not consent to his wish. But when he saw that Roughby was determined to go, he did what was asked of him, and went to the market to buy a sword. Instead of paying the price asked, he haggled and bargained for a price that pleased him. When the young man asked him if he had bought the sword without haggling, he had to admit that he hadn't. Roughby refused the sword and sent his foster-father back to town, begging him *not* to argue with the salesman. But the man couldn't resist. He was sent back a third time.

As soon as Roughby had the right sword, he ran to the edge of the lake and struck the water with it. His foster-father looked on helplessly as a fountain of blood spurted from the lake and Roughby vanished with a cry underwater.

Some Swedish farmers once captured a wild horse by slipping a halter over its head. The second the horse felt the leather on its skin, it was tamed. The men were able to use it for ploughing that day. Then the halter slipped from the animal's neck. In an instant, all its tameness vanished. The farmers suddenly had a rearing, snorting stallion on their hands instead of a plough-horse. They could not stop him from running to the lake and throwing himself into it, dragging the harrow along with him. Only then did the farmers realize that they had been ploughing all day with the Neck.

Several young men were on their way to a dance when they came to a river. It was swollen from the rains and overflowing its banks. It looked as if they would never get across. Then, as if in answer to their prayers, a horse appeared before them. Eagerly, the boys scrambled up on to its back, which lengthened to carry them all. They were about to guide the horse into the water when an old man saw them from the other side of the river.

'Cross of Jesus!' the old man exclaimed. 'What a long jade!'

The words were scarcely out of his mouth when he heard a loud crack! and saw the boys tumble to the ground. The Neck, his back broken, dragged himself howling into the water.

FOLLETTI AND INCUBI

THE Fauni and the Silvani were the first known Italian wood spirits. They had power over the fields and forests and made the flocks reproduce. The Fauni mated with the Faunae or Fatuae, and from this union the *Incubi* were born. These Incubi were originally herd sprites who gave the animals bad dreams. The Silvani married Wood Women or Silvane, and the *Folletti* were born. During the Middle Ages, the Incubi and Folletti were often confused. Today, the majority of Italian sprites are grouped together under the name of Folletti.[1]

Folletti were called Farfarelli by Dante, which means 'little butterflies', and, like butterflies, they never stop moving. They are usually friendly towards humans but at the same time can be very mischievous and annoying. They have the form and mentality of small children but are extremely interested in matters of sex and have many magical powers. Some rape and torture women, others are responsible for trichinosis in pork, still others can cause madness and give nightmares. They cannot be easily exorcized. Each town has its own formula for driving the Folletti away. Many of these formulas are exceptionally complicated. In Romagna, only brown-haired girls can make them flee; in other places, only great saints can exorcize them. Those who have been maddened by the Folletto in Lombardy should be given eggs to eat. One hundred and one eggs should be gathered from one hundred and one families and the sick person forced to eat twenty-five to thirty a day. At the end of five days the Folletto will be gone.

There is an almost endless number of names for the Folletti and each Italian town and village has its native elf. The Calabrian Fujettu loves to bother newly built houses in which seven families are living. In Sardinia, all unbaptized children at their death become Fuglietti. The Sicilian Fuddittu loses all his power if his red cap is taken away.

---

[1] To cite a specific example from northern Italy: the Silvani there were called SALVANI. The SALVANI mated with the AGUANE and their children were called SALVANELLI. The SALVANELLI slept with witches, and produced the Salbanelli.

Identification: Folletti are between one and three feet tall, with the exception of the SALVANELLI who can be as small as ten inches high. They often have curly hair and bright eyes, and love to wear red. Some have animal's feet, and the Aosta Mantellioni have no feet at all. Almost all have a magic red hood which gives them the power of invisibility.

Habitat: The Folletti live in Italy. Folletti rarely stop moving but, when they do, they rest in fields, light woods and houses. They travel in winds, and those who occupy themselves solely with the weather are known as WIND FOLLETTI.

A fifth-century woman of Pavia was in the habit of having her bread baked at the baker's.

One day she found a strange cake among the rolls. The baker said he didn't know where it had come from, so she took it home and ate it.

That night the woman was awakened by a strange hissing voice. She sat straight up in bed and turned on the light but could see nothing but her husband snoring beside her. As soon as she turned off the light, she heard the voice again.

'I *need* you! Come on, give me a kiss. Just a little kiss!' She felt lips brush her cheek but when she tried to push them away, found nothing there. She didn't sleep that night but stared at the ceiling repeating every prayer she knew a hundred times, while the Incubo continued to tempt her.

The next night was no better. He did all he could to seduce her, caressing her, whispering in her ear, threatening and coaxing her to come and sleep with him.

She went to the priest and was blessed and exorcized. She was given charms and holy water and told what prayers to say, but nothing did any good. In fact, the Incubo only seemed to bother her more.

One day he showed himself to her as a little man with golden

A Folletto

hair, a beard, green eyes and a fancy Spanish suit. She still refused to sleep with him. In his frustration, he became even crueller. He beat her, stole her jewellery and religious objects, upset the furniture, smashed dishes and then fixed them again, stole her child and almost threw him off the roof and walled her and her husband inside their bed. They were only able to escape the next morning because the cement was still wet.

The woman went to church and promised to wear a votive habit for a year as a penance. But the first time she put it on, the Incubo stole it from her, leaving her naked in the main street of town.

This state of affairs continued for six months. The woman was by this time worn out from lack of sleep but she still refused to give in to the Incubo's demands. Finally even his lover's patience was exhausted. He returned her dress and jewellery and went to look for another victim, most likely a woman with fewer scruples.

In many Alpine villages, jobs are hard to find in winter, and the young men frequently part from their families to work in the cities. Many men leave Val Varaita (near Novara), some after only a few months' marriage. Old women are put in charge while the men are away. Their most difficult task is caring for the new brides and protecting them from the fireplace Folletti.

As the winter wears on and the nights lengthen, loneliness overcomes the girls and they think of their husbands far away. Snow falls softly against the window and they move closer to the fire for warmth, but the longer they stay there, the more dangerous it becomes, for in the fireplace lives a tiny Folletto with burning eyes who slowly hypnotizes the girls. They sit before the fire and think of the city many miles away. Are their husbands with other women? The Folletto seduces them with his eyes and fills them with melancholy and despair. If at this

point the old women don't distract the young brides and if the
hold of the Folletto is not broken, the girls will shortly die,
lonely and broken-hearted.

mound folk

THE Norwegian Thusser were at one time so numerous that
they kept the early Christians from moving into Norway.
Today, the Christians have succeeded in driving a great
number of them out of the country and revile them as 'evil
Trolls'. Correctly speaking, the Thusser and all other *Mound
Folk* can only be called Trolls in a generic sense. The name
Trolls was used originally to loosely designate all the Scandinavian elves, whether wood elves, lake elves or Mound Folk.
Furthermore, the traditional picture of Mound Folk as misshapen, hunchbacked monsters who can only occasionally curb
their desire to sicken, murder and cheat human beings is a
completely erroneous one championed by amulet-peddlers who
sought to make a fortune selling charms to easily influenced
souls. In reality, the Mound Folk are tall, thin elves of great
age and even greater skill. They are the master smiths the Eddas
tell us about and are clever mechanics who know the secrets of
old runes. Their cattle are among the fattest in the land, and
certainly the best milk-producers. They live inside mounds
with all the typical characteristics of village life: dogs, children,
dances, quarrels and parties.

The working day of the Mound Folk begins at twilight and
ends at dawn. It is during this time that they fashion their
famous swords as well as sturdy pots and pans, costly bracelets,
knives and coats of mail. The women busy themselves with
brewing, baking, herding cattle, sewing and caring for the

children. But their favourite occupation is dancing. On warm summer nights or when the moon is full, they can be seen and heard dancing and fiddling with great joy. They are said to know the secret of the Elf King's Tune, music so sprightly and overwhelming that even the stones and trees must dance to it. To stop the dance, the fiddler must play the whole tune backwards or have someone cut the strings of his fiddle. The lusty dances of the Mound Folk continue all night, until the first cock crow in the morning. Then the dancers prepare to leave, since they know that if they are still there when the third cock crows, the early morning sunlight will change them to stone or turn their beautiful proud faces into shrivelled masses of dark grey wrinkles.

Identification: The Scandinavian and Icelandic Mound Folk are between four and six feet tall. Their women are exceptionally beautiful, tall and thin, with tinkling voices and long breasts. Men as well as women wear colourful peasant clothes, red, green or dark grey. As long as they do not come into contact with sunlight, the Mound Folk's skin stays a pale blue translucent colour. The minute one ray of sunlight hits them, their skin darkens, or they turn to stone. They can only be seen at high noon in direct sunlight, and they often take shapes other than their own. Their cattle also have pale blue skin, making them virtually invisible to humans.

Among the several subspecies of Mound Folk: the Norwegian Thusser, the Finnish Maanväki, the Norwegian Huldre Folk with their cow tails, the Faroe Island Hulde Folk and the Swedish shoemaking Pysslinger-Folk.

Habitat: The Mound Folk make their homes in Iceland, Norway, Finland, Sweden, Denmark, and the Faroe Islands. Although most Mound Folk live under hills or mounds, some prefer to stay under bushes in open meadows, under the roots of old trees, in caves or, as is very rarely the case, in abandoned houses. The Icelandic Mound Folk move once a year on New

Year's Eve. On this night and on other full-moon nights, it is possible to look into their mounds, raised on high red pillars.

A Dane was once on very good terms with his neighbour, a Hillman. They visited each other often and had long chats on the nature of man and the changing times. The first sign of trouble came when the farmer's first child was born. The farmer wanted to invite his friend to the christening but didn't feel he could, since the priest was so opposed to the old Hill-folk. If he invited the Hillman he would lose his good standing in the town and if he did not invite him, his neighbour would be greatly offended, and wouldn't give the child a christening gift. Try as he would, the man could find no solution to his problem. Finally, in desperation, he took his problem to the pig boy, who was supposed to be unusually clever.

'All I'll need is a big sack and permission to invite the Hill-man myself, and I'll guarantee there will be no trouble,' the boy told him.

The farmer agreed, and sent the boy off with a large sack. The pig boy knocked on the Hillman's door and was let in.

'I've come to invite you to the christening of my master's first child,' the boy told the Hillman. 'There will be a celebration and my master would be happy if you could come.'

'I'd be honoured to come,' the Hillman replied. 'But what sorts of guests are going to be at the christening?'

'Just the townspeople,' the boy answered, 'and a few priests!'

'Priests? Well, I suppose a few priests are all right. I could come a little later and sort of stay in one corner. Are there going to be any more guests?'

'Well, a bishop or two will be there and, of course, Peter and Paul.'

'*Saint* Peter and *Saint* Paul?' the Hillman asked.

'Who else?' the pig boy replied. 'And of course Mary herself will be there.'

The Hillman began to hesitate. 'I really would like to come but then I have much work to do, and the door needs mending. . . . What kind of music did you say you were going to have?'

'Drums.'

'Drums! No, I can't come to your christening! My leg was broken here years ago by a drumstick. Drums! Mary! Saints! Bishops! You'll have to tell your master that I'm sick. I'll send a christening gift along so he won't be offended. Do you think this will be enough?' asked the dwarf, holding out a king's ransom in gold.

'I don't know,' answered the boy. 'Maybe a little something more. He's used to rich presents.'

'Then here, take this, and please don't let them play the drums too loud. Is that enough?'

'Well. . . .'

'Here's some more, and send my apologies to your master.'

The boy thanked the Hillman and was barely able to drag the sack of gold back to his master's house.

Although the Huldre Folk work in iron and make razor-sharp swords and knives, they are frightened of steel and guns and must yield before them.

A man once fell in love with a Huldre Woman and decided to make her his wife. One evening he went to her hill and as soon as she appeared, ran up to her and held a gun over her head. The Huldre Woman could not fight against the power of the steel and was forced to go with him.

They lived together as man and wife for several years, although not in what one would call marital harmony. The elf-woman still resented the way she had been stolen from her people, and never missed an opportunity to remind her husband of her antagonism.

Even the birth of their first child was used by her to punish her husband. She walked over to the child as it lay in the cradle and said, loudly enough so her husband would be sure to hear, 'What a nice roast the baby would make for dinner!'

The man didn't find her remark funny.

'You devil-woman! And you call yourself a mother!' Beside himself with anger, he picked up a stick and beat her. 'You dare to talk about our child that way!'

But if the man had thought he could win a show of strength with a Huldre Woman, he was mistaken. His wife calmly picked up a poker and twisted it around his body like a piece of wire.

It was late summer and almost all the cows had left the high pastures. One girl had remained, herding her cows through the last warm days of the year. At night she slept alone in a little hut high on the moor, but loneliness didn't seem to bother her. Until, of course, the Huldre Folk came to visit.

She had just finished dinner and the last ray of sun had faded from the mountains when a knock came at the door. At first she was a little frightened, but then she gathered up courage and opened it. You can imagine her delight when she saw her fiancé standing in front of her.

'I thought you had to stay in the valley this week, and help your father prepare the house for winter. How did you get away?'

The Huldre Man who had impersonated her boyfriend answered, 'Well, I was so lonely that I decided we should get married, tonight!'

At first the girl couldn't believe her ears, but the Huldre Man's imitation of her friend was so good that she forgot all her fears and agreed to the wedding.

The wedding feast had already begun. The bride was decked out in finery and was drinking toasts to the Huldre Men who sat beside her, clothed in the personalities of the villagers, when her real boyfriend arrived, spurred on by some intuitive feeling of his fiancée's danger. When he saw the Huldre Men's black horses tethered in front of the hut and heard the sound of merry-making, he knew that something was wrong. Very carefully, he inched close to the hut and loaded his gun with a silver bullet. He shot over the heads of the Huldre Men and with the silver dispelled all the 'glamour' they had so carefully produced. Gone were the villagers and the bridegroom and in their place stood the Huldre Men in their true forms. Without a second's hesitation the young man picked up his girlfriend and leapt on to his horse. One of the Huldre Men tried to delay him by offering him a drinking-horn, but the young man snatched the golden horn from the elf's hand and galloped on.

The theft of their horn, as well as the loss of their bride, was a mortal insult to the Huldre Men. They untied their horses and gave chase to the thief. Both rode hard. Then the young man passed by some rivals of the Huldre Men who shouted out to him, 'Ride on the rough, and not on the smooth!'

The young man followed their advice and set off over the ploughed fields. Soon he had left the Huldre Folk far behind because they could not cross the uneven ground as easily as he could.

'We're safe at last!' the young man cried, hugging his girlfriend in relief. Then he saw his father's house burst into flames at the other end of the valley.

MER-WOMEN

THE *Mer-* or Sea-*Women* are the mistresses of the oceans. While their husbands visit the surface and occupy themselves with storm-brewing and weather-making, the Mer-Women herd and protect sea animals, collect gems and gold from the ocean floor and care for their children. They are impeccable housewives, managing hearth and land until their husbands' return.

Despite their industry and hard work, the Mer-Women's marriages are not successful. Almost all the MER-MEN are of advanced age, while the Mer-Women maintain their youth and good looks after many centuries and literally hundreds of children. The results are the same as in any other May–December romance: the Mer-Women soon search for more youthful lovers. Because of their relative isolation at the bottom of the sea, the Mer-Women must look for adventure to the surface, to the young men who sail the sea in hope of fortune and fame. The Mer-Women or Mermaids follow ships with handsome crews and sing sweet songs to entice them overboard. Once a Mer-Woman has set her sights on one man, she will not take no for an answer. She will wheedle, cajole, sing and call, often following the ship for hundreds of miles. If the sailor is not moved by her entreaties, she then devises a plan to have him washed overboard or has the ship wrecked, planning to rescue her young man and bring him to the soft beds of her palace. If satisfied, she may let the young man go, returning him to land with fine presents. But if the Mer-Woman is greedy, jealous or unsated, she will keep him a prisoner, refusing to let him see his loved ones.

Identification: The Mer-Women are more matronly than the RIVER WOMEN although nonetheless very beautiful. They live in the 'Land under the Waves' together with their husbands, children and cattle. Their skin is translucent and their supple breasts are thrown over their shoulders. Their hair changes from a dark green in the water to a blinding yellow in sunlight. The Mer-Women are often seen holding a comb in their right hand and a mirror in their left. They are excellent swimmers and enchanting singers and can also fly and change themselves into cats, seals, fish or fish-women. They are gifted with a very long life.

Habitat: Mer-Women are best known in northern Europe although they are also known in southern European countries under the name of SIRENS. In Scandinavia and northern Germany, they are called Havfrue, Meerweiber or Watermöme and their children are called Marmaeler. In Holland, they are known as Meerminnen. In Brittany they appear as Morgans and Groac'h Vor, in Man as Ben-Varrey, and in Ireland as Merrows or Mara-Warra. The English Mer-Women are known as Mermaids, the Scottish as Ceasg, Daoine Mara and Maighdean Mara. Their underwater palaces are of great splendour, decorated with gold, crystal and jewels.

A Mermaid from the Isle of Man was once caught in the net of a fisherman. His companions were in awe of her and her powers but nonetheless let the man take her home, thinking that she would give them luck with their fishing. The fisherman's wife was thrilled to see a real Mermaid. She pressed her to eat and drink and partake of their hospitality. The Mer-Woman refused to eat. She looked so unhappy that the family decided to let her go. They were too terrified of her moodiness to want her in the house any longer.

Once free, the Mer-Woman rushed to her friends and told them of her adventures.

'Did you know,' she confided in a hushed whisper, 'that those humans are so stupid that they throw away the water they use for boiling their eggs? They don't even know what it's used for!'

Her friends agreed that the islanders were indeed demented and broke off contact with them for many years to come.

It is common knowledge in Scotland that whoever catches a Mer-Woman is entitled to ask her for one gift before letting

her go. A man from Ross-shire was lucky enough to catch a
Mer-Woman while out fishing. It had always been his dream
to become a great piper, so he asked the sea-elf for the gift
of piping.

'Do you want to play,' the Mer-Woman asked him, 'to
please yourself, or is it for others that you wish this gift?'

'I suppose it's for myself,' the man answered. 'I just want to
be able to play the bagpipes.'

'In that case, I'll grant your wish,' the Mer-Woman said,
and slipped out from between his hands. 'But you will only
be able to please yourself with your playing.'

The fisherman became a piper, but only in his own opinion.
The other villagers had to cover their ears when he touched
the instrument. To them, his piping sounded like a chorus of
a hundred rabid alley-cats.

A group of Irish immigrants set off for America in hopes
of finding the Promised Land. But they had not sailed far
when one of the sailors sighted a Mermaid, following in the
wake of the ship.

'We're lost!' the man cried. 'A Mermaid at sea means
disaster. She's after one of our men, and will drown us all if
she doesn't get him.'

After much discussion, the crew elected to throw one man
overboard to appease the Mermaid. Lots were drawn. The
loser was a young Irishman, brawny and good-looking, the
most popular sailor on board. Saddened by their choice, the
passengers drew again, but the young man was singled out
once more. The man's strength, skill and good cheer were so
highly valued by the sailors that they gave him one more
chance. Lots were drawn the third time and he was chosen
once again. They then had to agree that he would satisfy the
Mermaid.

The sailor begged half an hour's grace from the captain.

It was promptly granted. He walked to the stern, looked the Mermaid in the eye and began to sing. He sang an ancient song in the language of his ancestors, a rich old Gaelic, full of memories of the past and of the sea. The words were truly old, for they pleased the Mermaid. Within half an hour, she was sound asleep, lulled by the waves and the old song of the young sailor. She did not trouble the ship for the rest of the journey, and all landed safely in the New World.

MER-MEN

ALTHOUGH all water is one in folk belief, and even inland lakes are thought to be directly connected to the sea, a distinction is made between fresh- and salt-water elves. The elves who live in fresh water are handsome young men who love to seduce mortals and play the fiddle or harp. The *Mer-Men*, salt-water spirits, have long hair and beards and are of great age. In the Scandinavian countries and in Scotland, Holland and Iceland, these differences are not so clearly marked, owing to the existence of hundreds of fjords and salt-water rivers.

The Mer-Men have, together with their wives the Mermaids, undisputed control over the weather at sea. They are responsible for storms, tidal waves, hurricanes and trade winds. Those who drown are taken into their homes on the ocean floor.

At one time, all ship captains were practised in the art of placating Mer-Men. The sea elves were given appropriate offerings and the bodies of the dead were entrusted to their care. Many verbal bouts were held between captains and Mer-Men, the winner being whoever got the last word in. In extreme danger, some captains even promised their sons or daughters to the Mer-Men in exchange for help. So important was the relationship between captain and sea elves that it was assumed that only a captain on good terms with the Mer-People could safely bring his ship through a journey. Such a man commanded respect and could wield despotic powers.

Identification: Mer-Men usually take the form of old men with long beards and green or fish-like teeth. They have the ability to take on other forms: those of men, bulls, fish-men, or fish. The fjord Mer-Men show themselves as horses with inverted hooves, half-horses or black stallions. In Scotland, these water horses or Kelpies have grown to such tremendous size that they deserve to be called giants rather than elves.

The Mediterranean Mer-Men have the upper body of a man and the lower body of a fish. They carry three-pronged tritons and ride dolphins. The Irish Merrows appear as fish-men with green teeth and hair and short finny arms. Their eyes are like those of a pig, and they have red noses from perpetual drinking. They travel through the water with the aid of a red cap. The Dutch Neckers spend most of their time sighing and are smaller than most Mer-Men. The Scottish Daoine Mara are hairy and bearded, have large mouths, flat noses, long arms, yellowish skin. All Scandinavian Mer-Men have long green hair, beards and fish teeth. The Havmand is somewhat younger and has a fish tail. The Nökke wears a green hat, has slit ears and only one nostril. Among the many other subspecies are the Söedouen, the Näcken, the Näkku and the Nikkur.

Habitat: Mer-Men can be seen wherever there is salt water. They make their homes on the ocean floor or in caves on the shore. Most live with their families in communal dwellings, but the fjord Mer-Men live alone.

Grethe often came down to the sea to look at the waves, and to wonder what lay beyond the vastness. One day she met a Havmand on the beach. He invited her to visit his house and promised to show her riches – more gold and silver than she had seen before. After a little hesitation, Grethe agreed and went with the Havmand. The riches of his house and his charms must have been great indeed, for Grethe did not return for many years. She married the Havmand, and lived with him in his underwater palace. She had five children and hardly thought of her old home or of the life she had left behind.

But even dreams must come to an end, and Grethe could not stay with the Havmand for ever. One day she heard church-bells through the deep water and became homesick. Her home-sickness grew and grew, until she had to go on land. Once home, she forgot about the life she had led under the sea, and the picture of the Havmand faded from her memory.

The Havmand did not find it so easy to forget her. Day after day, he waited for her to return and told the children not to worry. But one day he felt he had to cry. He cried for the loss of his Grethe and for the children she had left behind.

hobgoblins

THE BROWNIES are the most important Scottish house elves, the BWCIOD the most numerous Welsh sprites, and the *Hobgoblins* the most populous English species. They rarely leave the house, preferring to stay warm and comfortable next to the hob. Every section of England has its own neighbourhood Hobgoblins, and they are known under a variety of names. Hob-Gob, Tom-Tit, Robin Round Cap, Hob-Thrush Hob and Goblin-Groom were individual Hobgoblins so well-known that they were called by their proper names. Unfortunately, fewer and fewer English home sprites have been seen in recent years, owing to their distrust of crowded towns, electricity, machines and industrialization. They have become so rare that most people are only acquainted with them through stories and poems. Although Robin Goodfellow and Puck are perfectly

A Hobgoblin

respectable names for Hobgoblins, they are most likely not the names of historical elves but of literary personifications.

Identification: Hobgoblins are almost extinct and therefore it is difficult to find detailed descriptions of them. Usually one or two feet tall, they have dark skin and are either naked or dress in brown tattered clothes.

Habitat: Hobgoblins live by the fire and rarely go outdoors. At one time they were known throughout England and into the Scottish Lowlands. Today they are only seen in the most deserted areas where the inhabitants still adhere to the old ways of life.

A Herefordshire Hobgoblin used to have a peculiar method of avenging himself when slighted. He stole all the keys in the house and would not return them till begged to. The people in the house had to place a cake on the hob, and sit quietly in a circle around the fire, their eyes closed, until the sprite's anger cooled down and his hunger had been sated. Then he would throw the keys against the wall and the humans could go on with their work. After this, the goblin returned to his favourite spot on the horseshoe hung over the fire.

night elves

EVERYONE has at one time or another had a nightmare, but few seem to know that nightmares are caused by elves who ride their victims like mares. One of the most common symptoms of those afflicted with a *Night-Elf* is a feeling of helplessness: no matter how hard the dreamers try, they can't move a finger or even scream. It is, as one writer has put it, like having tetanus: a man is safe only if he can succeed in moving some part of his body. The elf sits on the chest or back of the sleeper and rides him through his dreams, his hands gripping his mount's 'mane' tightly. Night-Elves also ride animals, leaving their hair so tangled and matted that it is impossible to comb out.

There are two methods of keeping Night-Elves away: prevention and expulsion. In the Middle Ages, various plants such as century, Palma Christi, verbena and St John's wort were hung around the room to keep Night-Elves away and the sleeper wore amulets containing diamonds, coral, jet, jasper, dried menstrual blood or pieces of wolf's or ass's hide. In more recent years the preventatives have been somewhat simplified. Among those still used are: (1) a knife kept in the house at all times; (2) a horseshoe or a cross and a knife hung over the door; (3) flax thrown before the door; (4) a pig's head or pentagram drawn on the door; (5) excluding wax candles from the house; (6) mistletoe or a blessed olive or vine leaf hung over the bed; (7) a cross and crab-apples kept in the house; (8) a sock kept under the bed; (9) a twig of broom or a knife under the pillow; (10) shoes kept with the toes pointing away from the bed; (11) a red cloth tied to the chests of horses and of children; (12) crossing legs and arms before going to sleep. These preventatives vary from town to town and from county to county.

Once the Night-Elf has found his way into a house, there are many formulas to expel him. Catholics say the elf will leave if Jesus' name is spoken or a sign of the cross is made with the tongue. Others claim that the only way to scare the Night-Elf away is to pronounce his real name. Many charms can be said and the Night-Elf can be sent on many errands (picking up birdseed from the floor, spinning large amounts of wool, etc.). But by far the most effective method is to catch him. Because of his ability to change shapes, this can be quite difficult unless all his escape routes are cut off. If all the holes in a room are blocked, the Night-Elf will be forced to remain, since he must enter and leave through the same hole. If he is then wounded and loses nine drops of blood, is seized by his hair and told it is horse-hair, is captured with gloves that have been passed down in the family or is caught as a straw and then burned, he will not return. A curious method of catching the Night-Elf is to stopper a bottle very loudly. Partly out of curiosity and partly out of the overwhelming desire to urinate, the Night-Elf must open the bottle, making it easy to close him inside it.

Identification: The Night-Elves have many names and many forms. Because they appear in the dark and are shape-changers, it is impossible to give a definite description of them. They have been seen in the shape of women, as men, cats, chickens, monsters, donkeys, horses, butterflies, bats, mice, feathers, straws and horses' tails.

The INCUBI and some FOLLETTI act as Night-Elves, oppressing sleepers and causing bad dreams. However, true Night-Elves occupy themselves solely with sleepers, and only at night. Among some of their many names: Alp, Stendel, Waalrüter, Cauchemar, Nachtmart, Cinciut, Le Rudge-Pula, Marui, Painajainen, Marantule, Pandafeche, Shishimora, Schrätteli, Toggeli, Calcatràpole, Engue, Quaeldrytterinde, Nachtmännle and Schrecksele.

Habitat: The Night-Elves are common throughout Europe. Little is known of their activities during the day or where they sleep. They enter houses through keyholes or through holes or knots in the wood.

Several men were walking through a field in Holland when they saw a naked woman asleep in the grass. The men were at first aroused by the strange sight, but their enthusiasm was dampened by an old shepherd.

'If you think that woman is real flesh and blood,' he told them, 'you're sadly mistaken. She is the Maere, and is preparing to ride her next victim. She's more devil than any real woman!'

As the men stared at her, a small black insect or animal crawled into her mouth. She woke suddenly and in a few seconds was gone, running naked into the woods.

A Russian man was once tormented to such an extent by a Mora that he decided to abandon his house. Mounted on his favourite white horse, he rode until he came to a friend's farm. The friend willingly agreed to let him stay until the Mora had left his old home. But that night the host found his friend lying in bed, a tuft of white hair over his face, half-suffocating him. Without hesitating, the host picked up a pair of scissors and with one swift stroke cut the tuft in two. When the guest awoke the next morning, he found his horse dead in the stable. He now realized how the Mora had followed him from his old home – in the guise of his faithful white horse.

CALLICANTZAROI

THE *Callicantzaroi* appear during the twelve days of Christmas and take part in a long procession which winds its way through the Greek hills. They ride on lame, blind or otherwise deformed chickens, dog-sized horses and donkeys. They themselves are often blind and the 'lame demon' or Koutsodaimonas who accompanies them is a horror to behold. He is small but has a much larger head than his companions. His tongue always hangs out of his mouth and he has a big hump on his chest. His genitals are completely out of proportion to his body, and always visible. He refuses to ride but hobbles along at the end of the procession, cursing and mocking the rest of the company. When the cock crows in the morning or when the priest comes to bless the houses on 5 January, forcing the Callicantzaroi to vanish, the Koutsodaimonas holds out to the last, hoping to play some final trick.

Greek farmers arm themselves against the Callicantzaroi with fire, carrying lighted torches when they go outdoors at night. They also take special care that all water containers are tightly closed during the holidays. If they are left open at night, and there is no asparagus or hyssop in the house, the Callicantzaroi will contaminate the water or the fireplace with their urine. Near Mount Parnassos, they even go so far as to wash their genitals in the stinking water.

The lame demon is especially dangerous to have in the house, for he rapes young girls and shoves his horns into the bellies of pregnant women. To make sure that he stays away, a sieve and a broom should be laid by the door, some pork bones hung in the chimney and incense burned at night. A smelly but effective precaution is to burn bits of old shoes in the fireplace. No Callicantzaro can stand the stench!

Identification: The Callicantzaroi are the size of small children, skinny and always naked. They wear red hats and have little hair. Often blind in one or both eyes, many have a horse's or ass's foot. Larger races of Callicantzaroi are known in other parts of Greece, the last relatives of the Centaurs. These wood spirits are of enormous size and have been confused in the popular mind with werewolves and wild men.

Habitat: The Callicantzaroi are famous in the vicinity of Mount Parnassos. The lame demon is known throughout Greece, from Epirus on the west coast to the islands near the Turkish border. He has also been seen on Malta, and travels in the

A Callicantzaro with the Koutsodaimonas

company of the NEREIDES as well as with the Callicantzaroi.

The kingdom was in an uproar, for the Princess had been blinded by the lame demon. As usual, the Koutsodaimonas had lingered behind when his friends started to leave, and at the last minute had stabbed her in the eyes with his knife.

That night he had good news to tell his companions in their subterranean grotto.

'This time I really did it! The Princess won't ever see again, after what I did! Ha, ha! There's only one way she can regain her sight, and that's with soot and spider's webs from our chimney. But no man will ever find that out! Ha! Ha! Ha! You should have been there, and heard her screaming.'

Fortunately for the Princess, one man did find out. He had come into the cave in the late afternoon and lain down to sleep. When he heard the owners returning, he had quickly hidden himself and been able to overhear all that the lame demon said.

When the Koutsodaimonas and his companions left the next night, he came out from his hiding-place, gathered soot and cobwebs and set out for the capital. After many humiliations, he was finally granted an audience with the Princess. In a few days he had cured her completely. The King was overjoyed and rewarded him with an entire cartload of gold.

LUTINS

THE main thing to be remembered in dealing with *Lutins* is their capriciousness. One moment they help with the work, the next moment mischievously interrupt it, and then laugh at the whole thing a few seconds later. They are irrepressible and can think up endless games to pique humans. They transform themselves into stallions and, when mounted, promptly throw their riders into the ditch. They braid horses' manes and lock them up in pig pens, turn men into donkeys and scare hunters waiting for game. They appear as enormous spiders, lead people astray and attach two cows to the same side of the yoke. Some appear as goats, others as great balls and still others as fire. Some take the horns off cows, block roads and throw travellers off cliffs. Coast Lutins make seashells shine like gold nuggets and laugh as humans run to gather them. In some cases, the Lutins even let themselves be put to work as oxen to ruin the ploughing.

When in good moods, the Lutins can be quite industrious. Many stable Lutins pick out one horse as their favourite and feed and pamper it until it is the best-looking animal in the neighbourhood. They are very fond of children and play with them for hours on end. House Lutins warn of disasters, sea Lutins rescue shipwrecked sailors and coast Lutins guard fishermen's nets.

Although eccentric and occasionally malicious, the Lutins are seldom cruel. The only times they use violence are when humans disturb them at their work or spy on them. The unfortunates are then blinded, sickened or murdered.

Identification: The Lutins appear in a bewildering variety of forms and move incessantly from place to place. One Lutin, the Cula, is such a master shape-changer that it can choose between a thousand different disguises. The Lutins manifest themselves as small boys, animals, balls of yarn, giant spiders, small monks dressed in red, flying spindles, horses, men with wolf's heads, gusts of wind and travelling flames. The house and stable Lutins appear as small mischievous boys. Names used to describe the Lutins are almost as numerous as the forms they take. Listed under the house and stable Lutins are Moestre Yan of the eighteenth century, Petit Jeannot, Thomas Boudic,

Bom Noz, Sotret, Penette, Soltrait, Folaton, Fouletot and Natrou-Monsieur.

The country Lutins are called Lutins Noirs, Nion Nelou, Araignées Lutins, Moine Trompeur, Le Criard, Nain Rouge, Droug-Speret, L'Homme Velu, Cornandonet Dû, etc.

Habitat: Lutins have no permanent homes. Only the house Lutins stay in one place year after year and even then move when the owners move or when the master of the house dies.

The Lutins do not usually live next to running water, near rivers or mountain streams. They abound in stagnant waters, have been spotted near caves, visit moors and seashores, walk between dunes, travel over fields, live in houses and haunt dolmens and standing stones. They are natives of France as well as of certain cantons of Switzerland.

Two girls were once forced to spend the night in a stable. They were so tired that they immediately fell into a deep sleep, dead to the world.

When morning came, they found that a Lutin had visited them in the dark. Their hair was so tangled and knotted that it was impossible to comb out. All their 'lutined' locks had to be cut off.

It was customary in the valley to leave a bowl of milk every day for the mountain Lutin. In return, he would see that the animals came to no harm.

A herdsman began to be curious about this Lutin. He had never seen him, just heard stories about him. Besides, he did not believe that such a tiny creature could do so much to protect the sheep and goats.

One day, the man decided to take a look at the famous Lutin.

He carried the milk to the Lutin's eating-place himself and then hid behind a rock to see what would happen. After a long time, he heard tiny footsteps and saw a little hand reach for the milk. Before the herdsman could get a good look, he heard a terrified bleat from behind and turned just as his favourite white goat was crushed by a boulder. Before he recovered from the shock, the Lutin and the milk had vanished.

Nobody could believe his eyes: one of the most successful and sober men of the town was walking down the main street pulling a rope. The rope stuck straight out behind him, as if a great weight were attached to it. The man was pulling and heaving with all his might, the sweat running down his face.

'What have you got there, friend?' some of the townspeople shouted.

'If I didn't know you better, I'd say you were dragging the Devil to market,' another one laughed.

'You're not far from the truth, friend,' the struggling man panted. 'This Lutin has been driving me crazy, and I wanted to sell him to an out-of-towner. But the creature refused to come with me. Now I have to drag him away through the streets, making a laughing-stock of myself. I'll be so happy when I'm finally rid of the beast.'

Two fishermen on their way to Berneville came upon a young boy and offered to take him with them. He gladly accepted and entertained them with laughter and stories along the way. Just outside the village, the cheerful boy suddenly turned into the Nain Rouge and tossed one of the fishermen into the water. The other one, however, he could not touch. The Nain Rouge screamed at him in a thin strangled voice. 'You! ... You can thank your patron saint for making you cross yourself with holy water this morning. If you hadn't, you would have joined your friend in a surprise bath and not have spoiled all my fun!'

PIXIES

IN SOUTH-EAST ENGLAND, ants should be treated with respect. According to popular tradition, they are the last survivors of the original red-headed inhabitants of Cornwall. The children of these first settlers, and all other unbaptized or 'pagan' children since, change at their death into Piskies. At first the Piskies were man-sized. Accounts of them in the seventeenth century speak of them as being four feet tall. They then became successively smaller and smaller, until in this century they appear as diminutive Piskies or as Meryons, the fairy ants. It is believed that they will spend their last days on Earth as ants. Then they will never be seen again.

The present-day *Pixies* are tiny field sprites. They are hairy and naked, or wear raggedy green clothes and red hats. Mischievous and irreverent, they love to steal and to lead humans astray. They substitute Killcrops[1] for children, steal turnips and apples from the fields, sour the milk, lure men into bogs and laugh 'like Piskies'. They dance to the music of crickets, frogs and grasshoppers, and their dancing circles or 'galli-traps' can be found throughout Devon, Somerset and Cornwall. When they are in a helpful mood, they lend a hand with the threshing, pinch lazy maids and do the housework and spinning. Their help should be accepted quietly, for they depart immediately if thanked or presented with clothing. The house should be swept every night for them and a container of fresh water placed next to the fire.

[1] In German *Kielkröpfe*, or changelings.

A Pixy

Identification: The Pixies are between nine and twelve inches high, have red hair, pointed ears and turned-up noses, and are often hairy and cross-eyed. They are either naked or wear tattered green clothes. The Colt Pixy who guards Hampshire and Somerset orchards is not technically a Pixy, but a pixy horse who bites and kicks apple thieves.

Habitat: The Pixies are found in Cornwall, Devon, most of Somerset and eastern Hampshire. They are known as Grigs in some parts of west Somerset. They live under rocks, in caves, in small groves of trees or in meadows. Occasionally they will consent to live inside a house.

The Pixies, although normally solitary folk, gather together once in a while and hold large fairs. A poor Somerset farmer once passed through a pixy fair on his way home from market. The first thing he saw was a gold mug brimming with coins. Without thinking twice, he spurred his pony and grabbed the mug as he galloped through the fair. He didn't stop or look back until the house door was safely bolted behind him. He hid the gold under the bed and went to sleep dreaming of the good life he would now be able to enjoy.

His happiness was short-lived, for when he woke in the morning the mug had turned into a toadstool, and his pony was 'scamble-footed' for the rest of its life.

An Exmoor farmer lived in a village with several churches. He was in the habit of leaving some corn for the Pixies to thresh whenever he was short-handed. One night his wife spied on the naked Pixies through the keyhole, and decided to make them some warm clothes. Without telling her husband anything, she sewed shirts and breeches and left them on the threshing floor for the Pixies.

The farmer was furious when he heard what had happened. He knew that the Pixies wouldn't work for him now that they had new clothes.

Only much later did he see one of them again. The Pixy came to ask him for the loan of a cart and two pack horses. At first the farmer was reluctant. Then he agreed when the Pixy told him it was because 'I'd want to take my good wife and littlings out of the noise of they ding-dongs.'

The Pixy took the horses and moved his entire family over the hill away from the church bells. When the horses were returned, they were sleek and healthy and could do twice the work they had done before.

KOBOLDE

Kobolde are the oldest and most famous home sprites of northern Europe. At one time they were as common as mice and caused just about as much trouble. Priests preached against them and each parish kept an exorcist ready to ban them. Home-owners were either violently antagonistic toward the Kobolde or formed secret compacts with them, giving them shelter and food in return for promises of prosperity.

In very ancient times, Kobolde used to live inside trees. These spirit trees were later, as in the case of the KABOUTER-MANNIKINS, cut down and carved into figures in such a way that the tree's sprite remained inside the figure. These doll-like carvings were shut up in boxes, locked and brought indoors. Once indoors, the Kobold could not leave unless he was sold to another master. His new master could only sell him for less than he had originally paid and was the only one allowed to open the Kobold's box. If anyone else opened it, the Kobold would escape, causing no end of damage. Children were warned never to go near the Kobold. To teach them this lesson, toys were fashioned, housing scary Kobold-like figures, which survive today in the form of Jack-in-the-boxes.

As time went on, other ways were found of catching Kobolde and forcing them to come indoors. One method was to go into the woods on St John's Day and find a bird (the Kobold in disguise) on an anthill. The Kobold-hunter would then talk to the bird, catch him, put him in a bag and carry him home.

In recent years, Kobolde have come to like the easy life of fire and home so much that they now come into houses of their own free will. They are almost impossible to drive away. First they test the residents of the house by bringing in shavings and sawdust and strewing them on the floor or throwing dirt or cow dung in the milk. If the milk is drunk and if the shavings are left on the floor, the Kobold will know that he has found a place where he can stay. Once inside, the Kobold finds a dark corner for himself and sets up shop. He does the owners all kinds of favours and disfavours, and almost nothing can force him to leave. Many Kobolde stay on even after the house has burned down or follow the family to their new home.

Identification: Kobolde were originally one- or two-foot-high wooden dolls carved from mandrake roots or boxwood and enclosed in glass or wood containers. These figurines wore green clothing and had large mouths. One type of figure, the Monoloke, was made of white wax, wore a blue shirt and a black velvet vest, and went barefoot. In southern Germany Kobolde were known as Galgenmännlein, and in the rest of Germany as Oaraunle, Glucksmännchen, Allerünken or Alraune. The Galgenmännlein, Oaraunle and Alraune were carved from mandrake roots. The elves who lived inside these puppets often took their appearance but also presented themselves as cats, children or worms.

Today's Kobolde are the elves who once lived inside the figurines. They are around two feet tall, their skin colour

Kobolde

ranges from dark green to dark grey and they wear red or green clothing. They can no longer be enclosed in bottles and boxes but run wild, freely choosing their own masters and homes.

Habitat: Kobolde have settled in Denmark, Sweden, Germany, Austria and Switzerland. The name Kobolde has been extended by some to include all home sprites.

Now that the Kobolde are not kept imprisoned in dusty figurines they prefer to live in dark and quiet corners of the house: in the woodshed, the attic, under the roof, in the cellar, in the fireplace or in the barn. Occasionally a Kobold will live in or under a tree that grows near the house.

A man once passed by a small cottage and happened to notice the owner of the house, an old woman, digging in the yard. At first glance she seemed to be doing nothing unusual but then something about her, a certain air of urgency, made the man look twice. The woman was obviously very excited and kept glancing over her shoulder to see if she were being watched.

The man's interest was now aroused. He hid himself behind a bush to observe her more closely. The old woman went behind a tree and very carefully brought out a basket, lowered it into the hole she had dug and quickly covered it up.

The man was convinced that the basket contained the old woman's savings and could hardly wait to get his hands on them. He went home, fetched a shovel and waited until the old lady had left the house.

The minute she had gone, he ran to the place where he had seen her digging and uncovered the basket. Instead of the treasure he had hoped to find, he found a Kobold. No wonder the old woman had wanted to bury it! It stood about two feet high and had horse's feet, goat's horns, black skin and fiery eyes the shape of saucers. The man was so terrified that he ran away and caught a fever from the fright. The Kobold laughed and he, too, ran away. By the end of the week, the man was dead and the Kobold had vanished.

A Kobold made the life of a Körpenich farmer unbearable. Because the farmer was a religious man, the antics of the Kobold filled him with disgust. Nothing he did succeeded in driving the pesky sprite away. Finally the man's frustration reached such a peak that he decided to leave his house to the Kobold and to move into a new one.

The night before the planned move, the man was taking one last walk around his land, the land that he was now being forced to leave. He had not gone far when he recognized a familiar figure in the gutter.

'What are you doing here, pest?' the man called to the Kobold. 'I thought night was your favourite time for torturing innocent sleepers. What are you doing outdoors?'

'I'm washing my rags,' the Kobold answered, a little stiffly. 'I know you don't like my ways, but I've got to have clean clothes for the new house.'

The farmer saw there was no hope of ridding himself of the sprite. When the furniture was moved out of the house in the morning, the Kobold was given the place of honour on the cart.

leshiye and lisunki

SOUNDS heard inside a forest can be very confusing and misleading. This is especially so in Russia, where the sound of the wind, the echo, and the rustling of the leaves are all voices of the *Leshiye*. Men should refrain from listening too closely or the Leshiye, whispering and murmuring, will gain control over them and draw them off the path into the darkness of the woods. Once among the trees, men are at the mercy of the Leshiye. Sometimes they tickle their victims to death, sometimes they sicken them and sometimes they simply make them lose their way and then laugh at them.

The Leshy is the Lord of the Forest. All the animals in the wood belong to him and he can barter, sell or gamble them at will. He demands that all herdsmen who bring their cattle into the forest pay for the use of the meadows with offerings of animals or of milk. Like most sovereigns, he is surrounded by subjects, of whom the bear is the most important. He is the Leshy's servant and takes care of him when he has drunk too much with his friend the VODYANY.

The Leshy lives in empty huts in the forest. When a man is presumptuous enough to try to sleep in one of these huts, the Leshy reacts violently. He beats on the doors, howls in the forest and makes the wind whirl around the hut. In Archangel, a whirlwind is a Leshy dancing with his bride. In other sections of Russia, hurricanes are caused by fighting Leshiye.

Despite the great power the Leshy possesses, he is a seasonal lord and is only active from spring to autumn. In winter, when the snow blankets the forest, he sleeps, along with his servant the bear.

Identification: The Zuibotschnik (from 'cradle') or wood Leshy gets his name from his habit of cradling himself in the branches of a tree and laughing, crying, neighing, moaning, mooing, howling and roaring. He can be as tall as the highest tree in the forest or as small as the smallest leaf. He has goat's feet and horns, no eyelashes or eyebrows, only one eye, and claws. He is covered with green hair from head to foot, has grey skin and wears his sheepskin kaftan fastened the wrong

A Leshy

way round, without a belt. In Czechoslovakia, the Leshiye are called Lešni Mužove.

The field Leshiye are Leshiye who have moved to the outskirts of the forest and now live in meadows. Their height changes with the seasons, from the size of the stubble after the harvest to the height of the grain in summer. They, too, hibernate during the winter.

The Leshiye have wives and children, the *Lisunki*, who resemble them. In Czechoslovakia, their wives are called the Lešni Pany or Dive Ženy.

Habitat: Almost every forest in Czechoslovakia and European Russia has its native Leshiye and Lisunki. They sleep in empty huts in the forest and hibernate during the winter. The field Leshiye live in fields on the outskirts of woods.

The year 1843 was famous throughout Russia as the year of the Great Squirrel Migration. Tens of thousands of squirrels left their old homes in Vyatka to travel to new forests. Scientists were puzzled but couldn't explain the phenomenon. Among the people, though, there was no doubt.

A Leshy had obviously been the cause of the migration. The Leshiye are persistent gamblers and sometimes have to send their animals away as payment for their debts.

This particular migration was the result of a gambling bout between two Leshiye who lived far apart. The losing Leshy sent his squirrels to the winner, hundreds of miles away.

A woman was walking through the woods when she heard a baby cry. At first she was too frightened to investigate, for she thought it might be a Leshy trying to mislead her. In the end, her maternal instincts prevailed and she headed toward the sound.

In a clearing beside the path she found a child. It was shivering with cold and crying piteously. The fact that it was covered with green fur didn't stop her from picking it up, comforting it and warming it in her shawl. Soon the crying stopped and the Leshy fell asleep, happily cuddled in her arms.

Just then, the mother came running into the clearing.

'Where is my child?' she asked hysterically.

'Don't worry about him, he's sleeping peacefully,' the woman said.

'Many thanks for your kindness,' said the Lisunka. 'I thought I had lost him. Please take this as a reward.' She held out a pot of burning coals.

The woman was too polite and too shy to refuse the gift; she took it under her arm and started home.

When she arrived, she found to her surprise that the coals were not coals after all, but nuggets of pure gold!

'**G**ood day, sir, how do you do?'

'Not badly,' the stranger said, 'for this time of the year. Would you care to walk along with me for a while?'

'Gladly, I've been feeling a little lonely here myself.'

The two men walked together further into the forest. They chatted and gossiped and told each other stories. They had such a good time that the first man didn't pay any attention to where he was going. When he finally did notice that his companion's shirt was fastened the wrong way around, it was too late. He found himself in the middle of a swamp. His friend, safe on dry land, laughed fiendishly.

'You should *never* listen to a Leshy! Ha! Ha! Ha!'

The Leshiye are filled with new strength and vitality when they wake from their winter's sleep and often test their fledgling power against each other. When they fight, boulders and trees fly, the wind howls and the animals flee in terror.

During one of these springtime battles a Leshy was defeated by his companions, tied up and left in the forest to die. Just as he had decided that there was no hope, a merchant on his way home from market walked into the clearing, humming a song to himself.

'Good day to you, sir Leshy. I see for once that you're not causing any trouble! Ha! Ha! Ha! But I guess even you are entitled to your freedom!' The merchant pulled a knife out of his pocket, and in a few seconds the Leshy was free.

'Thank you for your kindness,' the Leshy said. 'You were on your way home, weren't you? Then let me help *you.*'

Before the merchant could say a word, a whirlwind had picked him up and carried him high above the trees.

'Help!' he cried. But he was in no danger. In a few seconds he was deposited safely on his own doorstep.

From that time on, whenever the merchant needed to travel in a hurry or had any errands to do, he called on the obliging Leshy.

people of peace

THE Little People of Scotland are proud and independent and can claim many distinguished ancestors. The Irish Daoine SIDHE visited Scotland in early times, as did the Scandinavian Trolls. They interbred and produced the present race of Sìth, the *People of Peace.*

The Sìth were in close contact with humans when the Picts inhabited Scotland, but in recent times have withdrawn more and more. Their relationship with men has become strained owing to misunderstandings on both sides. As is generally the case with elves, they respond well if treated kindly and badly if treated with disrespect. They sometimes steal children and often take farmers' cows for their dinner. Cattle should be protected from the People of Peace by horseshoes and crosses of mountain ash hung over the stable doors. Children should be baptized early and a piece of iron or steel kept in their cradles.

Identification: The Sìth are smaller and sturdier than the Irish Faeries. They are three to four feet high, handsome, have light brown skin and either blond or red hair. They love to wear green and have pointed hats. The Shetland Trows' hats are red, but their clothes green or grey. The Sìth speak old Gaelic among themselves.

Habitat: The People of Peace live in Elfhame, inside green hills which can be seen raised on pillars during the full moon. They are known throughout Scotland, and in Orkney and the Shetland Isles go by the name of Trows. They live in a different time-context from that of Earth. They are most often seen in May when they ride through the countryside in long processions called 'fairy rades'.

Two fiddlers were once approached by a hoary-headed man who told them he would pay them double to play at a party. At first the two were a little suspicious of the small, green-cloaked man, but greed won over caution. The small man led them to the top of a hill, stamped three times with his right foot and showed them into a large, brightly lit hall, filled with many little people dressed in green clothes and red pointed hats.

The fiddlers played merrily all night, and there was plenty of food and wine to go round. When morning came, they were paid handsomely in shiny gold coins.

'God bless you, sir,' the second fiddler said. With his words, the lights faded and they found themselves outside the hill. They walked into town but found it changed. The streets had widened and there were houses where there had been none before. They looked inside the church just as the preacher was blessing the congregation.

'In the name of the Father, and of the Son. . . .'

They saw their hard-earned gold turn into worthless leaves, and in a few minutes they, too, had crumbled into dust. That one night 'inside the hill' had in reality been one hundred years long.

The Beansìth, or woman of the Sìth, came every day. She would walk in without knocking, go over to the fire, take the largest pot from its hook and leave without saying a word. Luckily, the mistress of the house knew a spell to force her to return the cauldron: 'A smith is entitled to coals, in order to heat cold iron, a cauldron is entitled to bones, and to be sent home whole.'

Every night the Beansìth returned the pot, filled with bones.

This ritual went on for quite some time until one day the woman had to go to town. She left her husband in charge of the house, and told him to repeat the spell as soon as the Beansìth lifted the pot from the fire.

But the man had never seen the Beansìth and was so terrified when she came that he ran into the house and locked the door. That didn't stop the Beansìth. She simply climbed up on the roof and the pot rose to meet her of its own accord.

That evening the farmer's wife returned and was surprised

to see the cauldron gone. When her husband told her what had happened, she went storming off to the Sìth's hill to get it back.

There was no one inside except a couple of old men dozing in the corner. She tiptoed over to the fire and put her hands on the pot. She had almost made it out of the gate when the belly of the cauldron clanged loudly against the door-post. The old elves instantly woke up and called the dogs. Two enormous animals came out, one black and one green, and ran snarling after her. She threw a few bones from the pot to the dogs, and was safe for a few seconds. But soon the beasts gained on her and she had to throw more bones. When they started gaining on her the third time, she emptied the pot on to the ground and, with one last desperate burst of speed, ran into her house and slammed the door. She had regained her pot and the Beansìth never visited her again.

After a long walk, a man came to a field where some fat, healthy cows were grazing.

'Ah, if only I had some of their milk to drink,' he sighed, and went on his way.

A few minutes later, he met a small woman in a large green skirt who offered him a drink of milk.

'How did *you* know that I wanted milk?' he asked. 'And who ever heard of someone giving milk away? No thanks, you can keep it.'

The cow woman cursed him soundly for his rudeness, but the man didn't let it bother him and went on his way.

The next day, his body was found in a river a few miles from where he had first met the Beansìth.

An old Scottish ballad tells of Tam Lin the elfin knight:

Fair Janet, shut in her father's castle, had heard of Tam Lin and went stealing off to meet him. She found him beside a well in Cauterhaugh and stayed with him all through the day. The next time they met she looked him in the eye and asked, 'Are you a fairy lover or a Christian man? For I am pregnant and must know whom to blame.'

He replied: 'Janet, let me ease your mind. I am a man and no elf. My horse tripped while I was riding in the hunt and I fell into the arms of Elfland's Queen. Since then I have been a captive in their halls and have taken on some of their ways.

'But, Janet, if you want to save me, you can. You must come tomorrow, on Hallowe'en, to the crossroads and take me from my captors. I will pass by in the third procession on a white steed, my right hand gloved, my left hand bare, and my hair combed down in my face. If you take the horse by its bridle and hold me in your arms, I will be free. But first I will change into a salamander, then a snake, next a hairy bear and then a raging lion. Your right hand will burn as I become red-hot iron and then a glowing coal. You must hold fast and, at the end, toss the coal in water and cover me as I emerge, a mother-naked man!'

Janet did as she was told and held him through his changes until he stepped forth, her naked lover. When the Fairy Queen saw what had happened, she let out a scream and cursed him for his betrayal.

'If I had known you'd betray me, Tam Lin, I'd have plucked out your mortal eyes and given you new ones of elfin wood!'

BARABAO

THE *Barabao* is a city MASSARIOL, worldly and waggish. Women never fail to fascinate him. He loves to change into a thread, creep in between their breasts and then squeal in triumph, 'I'm a titty-toucher! I'm a titty-toucher!' When the woman looks down to see where the voice is coming from, the Barabao is already gone, making even more insulting remarks from another bosom. A few minutes later he can be seen trailing the week's wash through the streets or stealing bread from the baker.

The Barabao's curiosity is unbounded. He slips into bedrooms through the keyhole, lifting the covers to spy on lovers. He also hides in chamber-pots to peek at those above him. Not even the gondoliers can escape him. He impersonates people and then refuses to pay for the gondola ride, saying, 'Rickety-tickety tack, tomorrow I'll pay you back!'* He runs away laughing and clapping his hands.

Identification: The Barabao is usually two to three feet high but can change into any shape or form. He has a red cap, wears elegant red clothes, and is quite fat.

Habitat: The Barabao lives only in Venice.

A poor Venetian was on his way to work one night when he heard a crying sound. Lying inside an open door he found a small baby, shivering from the cold. He took pity on the child and carried him home. His wife lost no time in nursing the baby, dressing him in warm clothes and putting him to sleep in her son's cradle.

When her husband returned from work, he went to the cradle but to his surprise found nothing there. He searched all over the house, and then looked up and down the street, where he caught a glimpse of a red-dressed little man rubbing his hands together and laughing madly: 'She even gave me milk! Ha, ha, ha. The fool! Ha, ha! She took the Barabao into her house!'

PAMARINDO

A PARTICULARLY unpleasant northern Italian FOLLETTO is the *Pamarindo*. He is not only obscenely obese, but also lazy, and cruel to animals. When he travels down a road, he never bothers to step aside for anyone, but barges ahead, his bulk oozing and spreading until it takes up the entire road. The unfortunate traveller is often bowled over into the ditch.

The Pamarindo's diet consists solely of cow, sheep and goat meat, which he steals from local farmers. When he is hungry, he simply gives a long piercing whistle, and the animals run to him. They follow willingly when he starts off down a path, running faster and faster as he picks up speed. The Pamarindo runs until he comes to a cliff, then rolls into a ball and bounces over the edge. The animals can't stop in time and are smashed to pieces on the rocks at the bottom. The Pamarindo, happy with his success, can be heard far into the night, laughing horribly as he gorges himself on the carcasses.

Identification: The Pamarindo is two feet tall and very fat. He has pointed copper shoes and a copper hat, and usually wears red clothes.

Habitat: The Pamarindo lives only in Gemona, near Udine in northern Italy.

The Pamarindo

KLABAUTERMANNIKINS AND KABOUTERMANNIKINS

SAILORS, always superstitious, used to put great faith in their ships' figureheads. Not only did the carving have to be lifelike and magical, but the wood itself had to be very carefully chosen and cured. In the great shipbuilding centres of Flanders, the most treasured wood for this purpose was that of trees which had the souls of dead children living in them.[1] These spirits felt so much at home in their trees that they followed them even after the trees were cut down and carved into figureheads. When the figureheads were mounted on ships, these spirits took over the duties of the ship's sprite and warned of disasters, kept sickness away and helped the sailors with their work. They were in time given the name of *Klabautermannikins* and great care was taken not to drive them away. If they left, the ship was sure to sink.

Some of them did leave and took to the easier life of the harbour towns. As they travelled and multiplied, they became a common sight from Amsterdam to Copenhagen and were spotted inland, on the banks of the Elbe and the Oder. Many people told stories of these elves, now called *Kaboutermannikins*, who came into their houses on nights with no moon and lit warm invisible fires in the fireplace. The Kabouters often stayed for a long time in one home, helping with the house and farm work until driven away by gifts of clothes or by curses.

[1] It was the custom to plant guardian trees at the birth of each child. Such a tree's fate was intimately connected with that of the child. If the child died, his soul went to rest in the tree.

Land life has agreed with the Kaboutermannikins. They have become a little greedier and a little fatter and can frequently be seen in back streets, smoking their pipes. Some unkind citizens of Holland have hinted that they have become dim-witted since their move inland and that it now takes three Kaboutermannikins to do what one Klabautermannikin used to do. Even smoking a pipe has become a Herculean task. One Kabouter must hold the bowl, another has to hold a light to it, while the third pulls the thick sweet smoke into his lungs.

Identification: The Klabauter- and Kaboutermannikins are between one and three feet tall. They wear red jackets which are always a couple of sizes too small for them, and round red hats. Those who live aboard ship wear white or yellow sailors' trousers and high boots. Both the land and the ship sprites love to smoke.

Habitat: The Klabautermannikins live in ships' figureheads and travel with their ships down the Elbe and the Oder, through the North and the Baltic Seas to the Atlantic, and as far south as the Mediterranean and Adriatic.

The Kaboutermannikins live in mills and caves and upstairs in houses and castles, deep inside old wooden beams. They can be found in Holland, Belgium and northern Germany as far east as Leipzig.

The Kaboutermannikins of Löwen were once hired to build the church tower. The citizens were pleased with their work and rewarded them richly with gold and silver. The Kaboutermannikins were delighted. They had never seen so much money and took turns counting it, watching the coins glisten in the sunlight and letting them run through their fingers. The more time they spent counting their treasure, the less time they spent working, eventually shutting themselves up in their treasure chamber to devote more time to their hoard.

The days passed by and the weeks, and months and years. The Kaboutermannikins grew old, their gold locked up in chests and boxes, safe against thieves. A few Kabouters died but the survivors kept their unending watch on the gold. One day, the roof of their treasure chamber caved in, burying them together with their gold. Many have since tried to find it, without success.

It is a well-known fact that old men never tire of telling their story long after everyone around has tired of hearing it. Most of these stories go forgotten, no matter how long or how vehemently they are told.

'Once upon a time, I was a rich man, and not the beggar you see today. All my bad luck came from the time I swore at the Redcap who made me rich. What a fool I was! I've had to pay dearly for my rudeness, but the Redcap will never forgive me, and I'll die a poor man.

'It all started the day my wife fell ill, God bless her. She was a strong woman and had done all the housework for years, never missing a day. You can imagine how it was when she became ill! I'd never washed a dish in my life or been to market and suddenly there was no one there to do it for me. One night I was setting the butter churn in front of the fire when I saw the Redcap who was to bring me so much pain and trouble. But I didn't know it then, so I piled a few logs on the fire and tiptoed quietly around him as he slept there on the hearth with his bright red jacket and strange green face. That morning when I woke up, the butter was already churned, the fire was blazing and the kitchen was scrubbed and cleaned. From that day on, the Redcap did the work of three men. Even after my wife recovered, bless her soul, he stayed with us, tending the animals, cleaning the house, minding the child

A Kaboutermannikin

and washing the clothes. Every day he brought in firewood and lit the fires.

'I suppose the Redcap began to make life too easy for us. We soon had so much time on our hands that we didn't know what to do. I began to drink and my poor wife started to ask for more and finer clothes. But no matter how much we spent on clothes and drink there was always more. The work of the Redcap had begun to pay off. Before long, we were the richest people in town and could buy anything we wanted. The drinking and the wealth began to go to my head, for I became grumpy and nasty. I yelled at the children when I got home, cursed the dog and fell asleep in a drunken stupor. I can assure you, I was the most disgusting bastard in the whole town!

'Then I made my first real mistake: I yelled at the Redcap, and threw the firewood he was carrying down the well. With a wicked laugh, the little fellow vanished and I never saw him again. The next morning, things were as bad as the day he had come: my wife was sick again and didn't live through that week, may she rest in peace. All my savings had turned into potato peelings under the mattress, the cows died, the house was sold, and before I knew it I was a penniless pauper. If only I'd learned to curb my temper, I'd still be a rich man today!'

SALVANI AND AGUANE

THE marriage of the *Salvani* and the *Aguane* is a very serious relationship. In some sections of the Alps they are coupled under the names of Vivani and Vivene, Pantegani and Pantegane, and Bregostani and Bregosténe. They are the protectors of the lower Alps, the Salvani taking care of the trees and forests, their wives keeping the meadows fruitful and the stream water clear and pure.

Both are basically good-natured towards men, but react with savagery if anything under their protection is harmed. It is always advisable to ask the Aguana's permission before crossing through or bathing in mountain streams, and is even wiser not to touch the trees in the Salvan's part of the forest. If an Aguana surprises a man muddying her stream, she will either wrap her hair around his feet and then drag him underwater, or lure him into her cave and then rape or, in some easternmost sections of Italy, devour him. Women offenders suffer the same fate. Those who anger the Salvani always regret it. The forest man's long claws and his phenomenal strength cannot easily be forgotten.

Less is known of the habits of the Salvani than of those of the Aguane because the Salvani are rarely seen. They are so shy that they prefer staying in the woods in winter, covered with snow and ice, to seeking shelter in a farmhouse. The Aguane, on the other hand, have cultivated a real taste for men's company and travel down from the mountains to gossip, warm themselves by the fire and help with the housework. In the summer they can be seen in the fields helping with the haying, their long breasts thrown backwards over their shoulders to nurse the children in baskets on their backs.

Identification: The Salvani are of human size, hairy and strong. They have long, claw-like fingernails, and wear clothes of bear, wolf or wild bull skins. They are almost always hungry.

The Aguane are also man-sized and dress in furs. They are very pretty with long hair, sweet voices and drooping breasts. Their feet are either inverted or like the hooves of goats. The Aguane are shape-changers and present themselves often as ugly old women.

Habitat: These elves live in Italy, in the area bordered by the Brenner Pass, the Adige River and the Austrian and Yugoslavian borders, deep in the woods. The Aguane often live alone, rather than in the caves of the Salvani, in order to be close to running water.

A similar couple can be found in the French Pyrenees. The male is called Basa-Juan or Homme de Bouc, the female Basa-Andrée. In Spain, the male is called Ancho.

A man was returning late from work through the woods.

'Please, draw a circle around yourself!' a woman's voice cried.

At first the man was not sure he had heard correctly.

'Please, I beg you, draw a circle around yourself!'

Hounds could be heard baying nearby and the tone of the voice was urgent.

The man drew the circle with his stick. Just as he finished it, a beautiful young Aguana with pendulant breasts sprang into it beside him. The hounds, followed by the Wild Hunter Beatrik,[1] ran off into the woods and the Aguana was saved.

Tired from his day's work in the fields, a farmer fell asleep in the hay in his barn. He woke up abruptly in the middle of the night to see the moon shining through the boards of the barn.

'What a fine evening! What a beautiful moon!' he said aloud.

From outside the barn, a deep bass voice grunted, 'Yes, but it's night!'

The man groped for his scythe. When the Bregostano put his hand inside the door, he quickly chopped it off. With a howl, the Bregostano ran off into the woods. In the morning

[1] See note on p. 200.

the farmer found the hand lying there, a gold ring on each finger. He sold the gold and grew rich at the Bregostano's expense.

ENGLISH FAIRIES

THE word 'fairy' has been so often misused (especially by poets such as Spenser and Drayton) that it is very misleading to employ it as a scientific designation for a particular species of elf. The problem is further complicated by the many sub-species which go under the name of Fairies. The original, powerful majestic Fairies of King Arthur's time have inter-married with humans and other elvish races, producing a smaller, less powerful modern *English Fairy*. These can be seen throughout England, dancing merrily in the meadows on moonlit nights. During the day their night-time beauty is transformed and they appear as ugly, wrinkled dwarfs.

Because they are vain and don't like to be thought of as ugly, the Fairies usually appear during the day in the form of birds, cats, toads, or butterflies. The Essex Hyter Sprites are often seen in the form of green-eyed sand swallows. The popularized Dorset Fairies, Pillywiggins, are tiny flower spirits. Some, like the Lincolnshire Tiddy ('tiny') Ones, are tied to their native fens. Every dialect has its own name for the Fairies, ranging from Vairies and Frairies to the Suffolk Farisees and Lancashire Feeorin.

Despite their great differences in appearance, the Fairies still have many things in common. They all hate misers, St John's wort, salt, iron and rowan. They do not like to be talked about or to be thanked or rewarded. They will not visit a house which has ivy on the walls. Bluebells attract them, and primroses, four-leaved clover, cowslips and forget-me-nots give those with second sight a glimpse into their land. They love to dance, especially on full-moon nights in May. They usually treat humans well if treated with respect in turn.

Identification: The old majestic Fairies were Light Elves of large size and with fair skin. Like the Daoine SIDHE, they were aristocrats and came of the oldest families of elves. It is possible that King Arthur himself was one of them. They cannot be seen today, but are sleeping under hills, waiting for the time when they will be needed again.

The smaller modern Fairies are between a few inches and one and a half feet tall. They have become Dusky Elves. If seen in the daytime, they have old wrinkled faces. They prefer to wear red, but also wear blue, white or green according to the local peasant costume. They are shape-changers, and appear in many different insect and animal forms.

Habitat: They live underground or in great palaces above ground that can only be seen at night. They are known throughout England, although they are less numerous in the Midlands.

A little girl had wandered far from her friends while picking flowers. Clutching a nice bundle of primroses in her hand, she started home to show them to her mother. She walked and walked until she came to a large rock she had never seen before.

'But this rock isn't in the right place!' She looked hesitantly around herself and then wandered on until she came to another strange rock.

'Maybe this really isn't the way home.'

She sat down on the rock and the primroses, slightly wilted by now, knocked against the stone. She started crying.

'There's no reason to cry, little girl,' a voice said softly beside her. She turned around and saw many tiny Farises come out of the rock.

'But where did you come from?' she asked. 'And how did you get here?'

'We've come from another land, and your flowers opened our door. Here's a ball we've brought for you to play with,' they replied and handed her a large golden ball. She was delighted and laughed merrily as they accompanied her home.

A conjuror was at the house when she arrived and listened carefully to her story. He thought he could also get a golden ball for himself.

The next day he went to the meadow and picked an enormous bunch of primroses. He wasn't as lucky as the little girl, for he had gathered the wrong number of flowers and had come on the wrong day. The Farises who came out of the rock this time weren't gentle and kind, but very angry. The magician was never seen again. Most likely he still lives under the rock, 'taken' by the Farises.

Cakes that aren't marked with a cross before baking often get tiny pock-marks on them when set out to cool. The Somerset people say that the holes are made by the Vairies who dance on them with high-heeled shoes.

An Oxfordshire man had a fine apple tree. It produced the best fruit in the parish and never had an off-year. Many people came from miles around to marvel at it and all who came went away with a couple of apples.

One neighbour wasn't content just to look at the tree. He refused the apples the man offered him, but stayed awake at nights thinking how *he* might own such a tree.

One night he looked over into the farmer's yard and saw tiny lights in the tree and heard songs coming from inside its branches. Trembling with envy, he grabbed his rifle and went running out of the house. He fired straight into the middle of the tree. The lights suddenly went out and the songs stopped. A flock of tiny green birds swarmed angrily at him and pecked at his eyes.

That didn't stop greedy Jack. He didn't heed the warning of the fairy birds. The next night he took an axe and chopped the tree down. It fell with a crash to the ground, and the lights went out for good. Maybe he hoped that the birds would move into his own tree. If he did, he was sorely disappointed. His neighbour had lost the magic tree, but greedy Jack had lost his luck, and died a poor and bitter man.

SERVÁN

IN SWITZERLAND and northern Italy, misplaced objects are not lost by accident but have been stolen by the *Serván*. He runs away with the most useful items: keys, scissors, needles, pens and even spectacles. When his infuriated victim begins to swear and yell, 'Who's taken it?' the Serván laughs, fully enjoying the man's predicament. He then looks for something else to hide.

The Serván's pranks aren't limited to hiding things. He also pulls covers off beds, knots the tails of cows, binds oxen together in the same yoke, covers milk containers with moss or carries horses up on to the roof and leaves them there. A ram should be kept in the stable to protect the animals from his pranks and great care should be taken never to show anger at even his most outrageous escapades. If humoured he will help with the housework, take care of the animals and make

The Serván

the harvests more plentiful. All he will ask in payment is a bowl of soup or cream left on the roof every night.

Identification: The Serván is one to two feet high, dressed in red and has a merry boyish face. His laugh is loud and hearty. He is a shape-changer and appears as a goat, a dog or even a large ball.

Habitat: The Serván is known throughout the Swiss Alps and in the Basque Pyrenees. Because of the many languages spoken in these areas, there are many names for the Serván. He is called Jean de la Bolieta, Napfhans, Jeannot, Servant, Chervan, Folaton, Persévay, Sarván, Foulta or Le Patre. He is usually found in houses in small villages, close to the stove. Unlike his Italian relative the SALVANEL, he is primarily a home sprite and is included among the house LUTINS.

A miller once lived in the Italian canton of Switzerland, and was plagued by the Servant. The sprite was such a nuisance that the poor man was afraid to leave his mill for more than a few minutes at a time. As it was, he had already found several sacks filled with leaves and sand in place of his flour.

The Servant gave him no rest, laughing, playing practical jokes, making noises in the night, and giving the miller a hard time. But the man just laughed merrily at all that happened, never losing his temper, even at the most annoying capers.

Finally the miller's good humour won out. The Servant tidied up the mill and became his helper.

NISSEN AND TOMTRÅ

IN SWEDEN, it is often said that the 'groom lays the food in the crib, but it is the Tomte who makes the horse fat'.* The *Tomtrå* not only care for the horses and cattle; they are responsible for the well-being of the entire house. A home with a happy Tomte can easily be recognized by its orderliness and cleanliness. The Tomte is, furthermore, in charge of the finances of his family. He steals hay, milk, grain and even money for his masters and fights with other elves bent on theft. He does all the work of a hired man, sweating in the fields, washing the dishes and caring for the animals. He may even teach his favourites the art of fiddling.

Like most sprites, the Tomtrå and *Nissen* will not accept regular wages for their work but do make certain demands on their employers. The house and grounds must be kept clean and neat at all times or the sprite will leave in disgust, taking all the luck of the place with him. All loud noises and irregularities are forbidden, as is chopping in the yard. Holidays must be rigorously observed. At Christmas time, the home sprites should be given an extra gift of tobacco, a little piece of grey cloth and a shovelful of clay. Special attention should be paid to them on Thursdays when they have their weekly holidays; their food rations should then be larger than usual and an extra dab of butter put into their porridge. No one should spin on that day and all unnecessary noise should be avoided. In some sections of Sweden, the Tomte must be fed at ten in the evening and once again at four in the morning. The family that can manage to keep their Tomte well-fed and happy need never worry about debt and bankruptcy.

Despite the Nissen's and Tomtrå's capacity for hard work,

they are also fun-loving sprites and delight in dance and play. Their favourite dancing times are full-moon nights when the moonlight frosts their haunts with a silver shimmer. They then skate on frozen lakes and rivers.

Inside the house, their playfulness is taken out on humans and cattle. They box people unexpectedly on the ear, pull the hay away from dairy maids, tease young boys, laugh hysterically at misfortunes, dance, sing, pinch sleepers and let the cows loose in the winter.

Identification: The most common Finnish home sprites are the Tontuu and Para. In Russia they are called Maciew, in Norway Tomtevätte, in Sweden Tomträ and in the Faroe Islands Niägruisar. Nissen god Dreng are the Danish and Norwegian home sprites, and in northern Germany they are called Nisken.

Despite their many names, these northern house elves are very similar to one another in appearance. They have good figures and are extremely strong. They are as tall as a small child but their faces are old and wise and speak for their great age. Their heads are large, their arms long and their eyes bright. Many say that their laugh resembles that of a horse. The Nissen and Tomträ are most often seen wearing peasant shoes or soft slippers, red stockings, short breeches and grey or green jackets. In summer, they either go naked or wear jackets of rough cotton, and in winter their coats are of heavy wool. They are seen at noon or at night.

Habitat: Although Nissen and Tomträ originally lived in trees (preferably ash, linden or elm) they have now moved indoors. Their favourite spots are the dark corners of the house, stable, barn or woodpile. They live in northern Germany, in Denmark, Sweden, Norway and Finland, along the Baltic Coast and in the Faroe Islands, and have been spotted in some communities in North America.

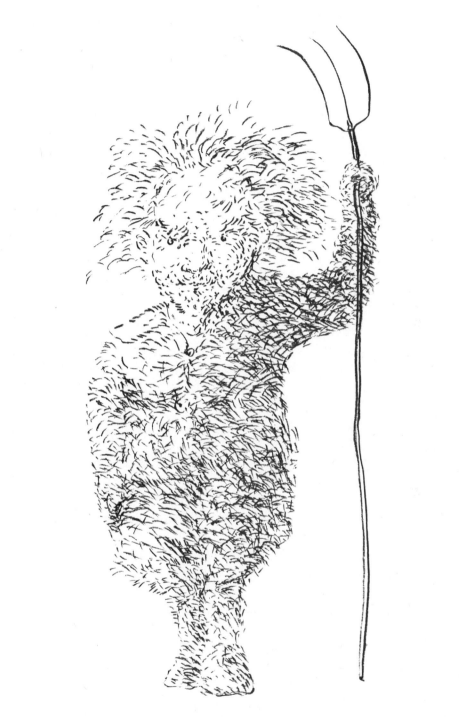

A Nis or Tomte

A boy once offended his family's Nis by threatening him with a pitchfork. The Nis did not take his revenge that day but waited for night-time, when the boy was safely asleep. He crept into his room, picked the sleeping boy up and carried him into the yard. With no apparent effort, the Nis threw the boy over the house eight times before tiring of the sport and letting his victim fall into the gutter.

Because of similarities in their characters, young boys and Nissen often quarrel. A Jutland boy and a Nis quarrelled more often than most. If the boy treated the Nis well for an hour, that would be the hour the Nis chose to torment the boy. The previous day, the boy had given the Nis his porridge but had hidden the butter in the bottom of the bowl. When the Nis did not see the butter, he began to fuss and fume, vowing to punish the boy for his oversight. Even when he *did* find it, he did not change his mind.

That night he went into the room where the boy was sleeping in the same bed with the master of the house. After pulling the covers down, the Nis studied the two of them for some time. Then he grabbed the boy and dragged him to the foot of the bed so that his feet were on a level with the man's feet. But that didn't satisfy the Nis.

'Long and short don't match!' he said, and took the boy by the head and pulled him to the top of the bed so that his head was on the same level as the man's.

'Long and short don't match!' he repeated, and dragged the boy to the bottom of the bed. This ritual went on all night. Needless to say, the boy did not feel very refreshed when he woke up in the morning.

Later that day, the boy got his chance to continue the feud. When he walked into the hay loft, he saw Nis sitting at the other end, his legs hanging over the edge, teasing the dogs in the yard below. The boy crept very quietly up behind the Nis and pushed him off into the greedy jaws of the hounds.

GIANE

THE *Giane* are the most numerous Sardinian elves. The first Giane were wood spirits, like the north Italian AGUANE, tall, beautiful women with long breasts who lived in caves in the hills and occupied themselves with spinning and embroidery. They could foretell the future, and knew where treasures were buried. Despite their many gifts and great beauty, they had difficulty finding mates. There were few wood men, the dwarfs were too small to interest them and the giants were rough, inconsiderate brutes. The lonely Giane passed their time working in their caves and singing songs. With time, they became master weavers, and could fashion fantastic white veils that covered entire valleys. Their songs, too, became something special, rich sweet lullabies that enchanted humans and drew men to their caves. The love-sick Giane had by now lost all desire for normal sexual relations and pounced on the poor men like spiders on their prey, killing them and sucking their blood. After three days, the sated Giane gave birth to children, small half-breeds with a taste for raw meat.

The present-day Giane have little to do with their blood-thirsty ancestresses. They are small and wear furs or gaily coloured peasant clothes. The men and women live together in well-furnished caves and eat wild herbs and meat. They are still fantastic weavers and can sometimes be heard singing enchanting songs.

Identification: The original Giane were five feet tall, with long wild hair, steel fingernails and long, long breasts which they threw over their shoulders. They dressed in furs and kept their children in baskets on their backs.

The shy descendants of these Giane are ten inches tall, have gold jewellery and brightly coloured clothes. The men often dress in furs and the women like to wear kerchiefs.

Habitat: The Giane live in Sardinia, in caves in cliffs, forests and hills.

seal people:
sea crows
and roane

THE *Sea Trows* of Shetland are close relatives of the land Trows. They are sometimes called Selkies or seals, for they cannot travel through the water in their own forms but must put on a seal or fish skin.

They come to shore on full-moon nights and dance on the rocky beach. If a man steals one of their skins, the Trow to whom it belongs follows him until he consents to give it back. Female Trows even marry the man in order to regain their skin.

Seal Women can easily be recognized when in human form by the slight web between their fingers, the roughness of their palms, their slow breathing, their fondness for swimming and diving, their fertility, their knowledge of medicine and mid-wifery and their ability to foretell the future. Although they make good wives, they never lose their love of the sea and return to it as soon as they regain their skins.

A Giana

Identification: The *Seal People* include the Sea Trows, who are frequently seen in the form of seals (in Orkney known as Haaf-Fish) with startlingly bright eyes. When they take fish form, they have green hair and scales. They are very beautiful and of human size when on land. The other Seal People, the Highland *Roane*, are gentle and shy and only appear as seals.

Habitat: The Seal People are seen in Scotland, Orkney and Shetland, as well as in Ireland. They live by preference under the sea but, if forced to, can live on land. Their underwater palaces are fine airy edifices of pearl and coral.

A group of Shetland seal hunters landed on a rock in the North Sea. They had killed many seals but still not skinned all of them when the sea started rising and the waves began beating against the rock.

'We'll have to leave now and forget the seals,' shouted their leader. 'All men to the boat!'

They didn't notice that one hunter had been left behind. He was frantic when he discovered himself alone on the rock.

'Hello! Is anybody there?' There was no answer. Then he saw that he wasn't alone. Some Trows were trying to revive the dead seals.

'My son! My son! Why did they have to take *your* skin away?' one female was crying.

Then she spotted the hunter.

'You're the one! You killed my son!' she shouted at him. Almost before he could answer, her fury gave way to hope. 'Then maybe you can bring him back to life again. If I can get his skin back, he will be saved. You must help me.'

The hunter promised to do what he could. The Trow mother turned into a seal and he climbed up on her back, cutting slits in her sides to make stirrups for himself. She took him back to land.

True to his word, the man found the skin and brought it back to her. She thanked him heartily and swam away, the wounds in her sides bleeding as she swam.

laúru

THE *Laúru* is the most handsome Italian FOLLETTO, very small with a perfect figure. His eyes are black and shiny and twinkle merrily, his hair is long and curly, and his clothes are made of the softest velvet. During the day he is rarely seen, preferring to do his mischief at night. He does not work in the house for fear of ruining his fine clothes, and only feeds those animals he likes. He loves women and always tries to seduce them. If rejected, he gives the woman nightmares until she hangs a pair of bull's or ram's horns over the door or yields to him. Whether the horns suggest to him that he is being cuckolded, or present a physical threat, is not certain. In either case, they will force him to leave the house.

The Scazzamurieddu is a Laúru who only lives in Lecce. He is slightly smaller than the Laúru and wears a red cap instead of the Laúru's sugarloaf hat. He is extremely mischievous, particularly with children, but can bring great fortune to a family by showing them the location of hidden treasures or telling them winning lottery numbers.

Identification: The Laúru is less than two feet high, has black eyes and black curly hair, and wears velvet clothes and a sugarloaf hat. The Scazzamurieddu is often as small as one foot high and wears a red cap, his most precious possession.

Habitat: The Laúru lives in southern Italy, in Puglia. The Scazzamurieddu is only found in Lecce. Both are home sprites.

A Laúru once appeared to a group of people and asked them if they would rather have a bag of money or a bag of broken pottery.

In unison they replied, 'Money, of course!'

The Laúru handed them a sack. When they looked inside it, instead of the money they expected, they discovered only broken shards.

ROOSTERS, SNAKES AND BASILISCS

IN MANY countries, house spirits appear in the form of *snakes* or *roosters*. The rooster elves appear most often in eastern Europe. The best-known is the Rarash. The house snakes were well-known in Classical Greece, and are still honoured in Yugoslavia and some sections of Russia. Westerners are more familiar with the offspring of magical roosters, the Salamanders of alchemical fame and the *Basiliscs*.

In folk belief, it is entirely possible for roosters to give birth. Understandably, these are no ordinary chickens but magical hermaphrodites with fiery eyes and fiery talons. The eggs that they lay must mature for seven years before hatching. What then emerges is a Salamander, held by Paracelsus and the alchemists to be the incarnation of fire, or the famous Basilisc, whose glance is powerful enough to kill a man.

Any Basilisc can kill and will continue to kill if not stopped by magical means. If a man can look at a hatching Basilisc before it sees him, then he will succeed in killing it, but if he loses the contest he must die. If the Basilisc is already full-grown, there are several methods of getting rid of it. One is to call it by its name, another to touch it with a branch of a special tree. But by far the most effective method is to hold a mirror in front of it, so that it can kill itself.

A lesser-known French snake elf is the Vouivre who appears beside fountains as a winged snake with a diamond in its forehead. This diamond is its only treasure, and is protected with great ardour. The only time the Vouivre lets the diamond out of its sight is while drinking or taking a bath. The man who succeeds in stealing the jewel will gain tremendous power and wisdom. The Vouivre, robbed of its treasure, will pine away, finally dying of blindness and loneliness.

Identification: The Rarash appears as a small boy with claws or as a black hen, as does the Lithuanian Aitwaras. The Hungarian Lidercz prefer to show themselves as hermaphrodite hens. They can travel easily through fire and air.

The Greek Stoicheioi are lazy spirits who are usually seen as snakes curled up under the fireplace. The Russian Tsmok is a house snake responsible for lightning; the Idrian Zmaj a house snake who appears as a rooster.

Among the western European sprites are the Basilisc, the Cocadrille – a very long, thin serpent with paws that are deadly to cattle – the Souffle, the Lebraude, Enfleboeuf and the Salamander. The Vouivre appears as a winged serpent covered with fire, a diamond in its forehead.

Habitat: The eastern European house roosters live exclusively indoors, as do the southern house snakes who are most often found sunning themselves on the floor or seen gliding into hiding places under foundation stones. The Basilisc is known in France, England, Portugal, Spain and Italy, and lives in the vicinity of springs and fountains. The Vouivre is a native of Gascony, the Cocadrille of the central region of France.

A drunken servant on the Greek island of Zakynthos once pushed his luck too far: in a fit of madness, he picked up a meat spit and speared his master's house snake. That year things went badly in the house, since the guardian snake was no longer there.

The anniversary of the murder drew near. That night the servant was drunk again. He started swaggering and boasting, telling of his bravery in killing the 'evil' snake. This was too much for the other servants. They argued with him. Words came to blows. Suddenly one of them picked up the spit and savagely ran the man through. It was a year to the very second since he had killed the house snake.

A poor farmer once found a black hen shivering under a pear tree. Surprised at seeing a hen alone in the forest, he picked her up, tucked her under his arm, and carried her home. That night he discovered just what kind of animal he had found. She flew into the house through an open window, a basket of potatoes in her beak and flames streaming behind her.

'Where did you steal that stuff?' he yelled. 'Take it back! I won't have any thieves in my house!'

The hen pretended she hadn't understood, and fluttered back to her roost in the barn. In the next few days, she brought the farmer gifts of wheat, rye and barley.

When the neighbours complained that they were missing grain, the farmer returned the stolen goods.

One day a neighbour caught the hen red-handed. He screamed at her and beat her with a stick. The hen fought back and, in a few seconds, the man was howling in pain, the hen perched on his back, beating him with his own stick and yelling, 'I am Rarash! I am Rarash! Rarash!'

Several other incidents occurred until the man who had found the hen decided to move. He considered it the only way

A Basilisc

to free himself from the Rarash. He packed all his belongings and then set the house on fire, hoping to burn the hen with it. You can imagine his anger when he heard a familiar voice squawking behind him, 'We're moving away! We're moving away! Soon we will be stealing somewhere else! We're moving away!'

Rarash's manners didn't improve in the new home. She stole incessantly, beat the servants when they didn't feed her and made a horrible nuisance of herself. Finally the man could stand it no longer. He went down to the chicken coop and pleaded with the hen not to destroy his life.

'Do I have to commit suicide? Is there no way you'll leave of your own free will?'

'If you still remember where you found me and take me there at exactly the same hour and day, I will leave.'

Without having to be told twice, the man did what she said, and never saw Rarash again.

moss people

STERN upholders of the old ways of life, the Moss Maidens insist that humans follow three simple rules: no one should peel the bark off a tree, bake caraway seeds inside bread, or tell their dreams. Men who follow this advice and who keep a strict old-fashioned household may gain the Moss Maidens as helpers. They bring great luck if they are properly fed or if the dumplings are never counted in the pot and the water is allowed to drip on to the floor so that they can help themselves.

The Moss Maidens are not only industrious workers and good housewives but also have secret knowledge. They know the healing properties of all the plants in the forest and show their favourites how they should be used. They know where to find the blue analgesic flower, ache-no-more, which is of special aid to women during childbirth, and they can cure most fatal diseases. The Moss Maidens make the crops grow better by dancing in the fields, and can easily turn leaves into gold. They are even generous with complete strangers, leaning down from their tree-nests to hand them a ball of yarn. No matter how many sweaters are knitted from the wool, it will never come to an end.

Identification: The Moss and Wood Maidens are between two and three feet tall. They are clothed in moss, so well camouflaged that they often can't be told from the trees around them. Their faces are old and furrowed, their bodies hairy and their skin is grey. They spin and weave all the moss in the forest, as well as their own clothing. They are ruled over by the Buschgrossmutter or 'bush-grandmother', a white-haired Dusky Elf who is as old as the hills and whose feet are as mossy. Among the many subspecies of Moss Maidens are the Flemish Moswyfjes, the German Lohjungfern and the Bavarian Finzweiberl. The Finzweiberl wear wide-brimmed hats and have spotted skin.

The male *Moss People* and Forest Fathers are very rarely seen. They are closely related to the Tirolean NORGGEN and wear moss-coloured clothes faced with red, and dark three-cornered hats. They are bad-tempered and should be avoided if at all possible.

Habitat: Moss Mannikins and Forest Fathers live only in virgin forests and are very difficult to see, but the females are easily spotted by woodcutters. They raise their children in moss cradles high in the trees, never venturing far from their birth-groves. They live in the woods of central Europe, from the Alpine fir forests in the south to the Bavarian forest in the east, into Poland and Czechoslovakia, and as far west as French Flanders.

A poor man on his way through the forest met a tiny Waldweibchen struggling with a broken wheelbarrow. The man was in no hurry and was, moreover, a fairly good carpenter. He set to work and before long had the wheelbarrow back in working order. The tiny lady was delighted and, as a sign of her gratitude, gave him the splinters that had fallen to the ground. Careful not to offend her, the man pocketed them and went on his way. As soon as he was out of her sight, he threw the splinters in the grass.

The next morning, as the man cleaned out the pockets of his coat, he found one of the Waldweibchen's splinters: it had stuck in the lining and had changed overnight to pure gold! The man never saw the Waldweibchen again and never found her other presents.

TREE ELVES

A SOMERSET saying, 'Ellum do grieve, Oak he do hate, Willow do walk, if Yew travels late',* does not specify the trees but the elves that inhabit them. The elm, oak, willow and yew are the homes of elves, as are the fir, holly, pine, ash, cherry, laurel, nut, apple, birch and cypress trees. Because each elf is born directly from the tree, he takes on its characteristics. For example, the Bodach na Croibhe Moire is pictured as a strong little old man, as gnarled and as stout as his parent oak. The One with the White Hand is a skinny white female born of the birch tree. But although many trees are the homes of elves, the elder has without doubt the highest elf population. The fruit-bearing trees are the homes of the Elder Mother, the Hyldeqvind and Frau Holunder, while the male trees house the grumpier male sprites: the Prussian Puschkait and the English Owd Lad. Under the tree roots live many tiny elves such as the German tree-dwelling KOBOLDE, and the Russian Barstukken and Markopolen who come under the supervision of the Puschkait.

Because the elder elves' lives are tied to those of their native trees, they act protectively towards them. It is safest always to ask their permission before cutting a branch or even picking elderberries. In Germany, before breaking a branch one should say aloud three times, 'Frau Ellhorn, give me some of your wood, and then I will give you some of mine when it ripens in the forest,'* and spit three times. The consequences of mistreating an elder tree, of breaking a branch without permission or of cutting down the tree, are often very serious. The Elder Mothers and Fathers have various means of avenging themselves. The person who cut the tree will lose his eyesight or his health or, as is most often the case, his children, his cows or his chickens will suffer.

If this happens, there is only one course of action: charms and offerings must be given to the wounded tree. When a child has been sickened by an angry elder elf, one should offer the tree wool and bread, and then address it: 'You Elders and Eldresses, here I bring you something to spin, and something to eat. Eat and spin, and forget my child!'* In most cases, the distracted elves will then leave the child alone.

Identification: The *Tree Elves* vary widely in shape and size as well as sex and clothing according to the nature of their parent tree and the severity of the climate.

Habitat: Tree spirits are known throughout the world and Europe is no exception. The Lithuanians, Italians, Germans, Finns, Danes, English, Greeks, Swedes, Spanish, French, Slavs and Poles all speak of native tree sprites, whether they are called Bodach na Croibhe Moire, Rhagana or Frau Ellhorn. The elder-elves are best known in the German and

Scandinavian countries but occur as far away as the Pyrenees and are very powerful in England and Wales.

The tree elves prefer fruit-bearing trees but have been known to live in others. Among the many species of tree elves should be included the Polish Boruta, a fir sprite, the Finnish Tuometar, a cherry-tree elf, Hongatar and Katajatar, the Danish Löfviska, the English nut sprites Melch Dick and Churn Milk Peg, the lascivious Rhagana and the Greek tree-living NEREIDES.

A successful Derbyshire farmer vowed that the cause of all his prosperity was the three trees that stood on a hill behind his house. Each year on Midsummer's Eve, 21 June, he climbed the hill and laid primroses at the foot of each tree.

Even on his deathbed, the old man didn't forget his duty to the three trees, or the Green Ladies, as he called them.

'My sons, no matter what you do, don't forget to lay the primroses at the foot of the Green Ladies every June. I beg you, don't forget it!'

The two eldest sons refused to listen to his advice. They considered the old man a superstitious fool and thought themselves much too manly to do something as degrading as picking flowers. But the youngest son was more obedient than his brothers. That June, he climbed patiently to the top of the hill and laid the primroses at the foot of each tree, just as his father had told him to do.

Many years passed, and each year the younger brother paid homage to the Green Ladies. This persistent obedience angered the older brothers. That June, one took an axe and chopped down a Green Lady. He died a little later.

The next year the second brother also chopped down a Green Lady. Before long, the youngest brother was left alone with the remaining tree. He continued his pilgrimages to the lone tree each Midsummer's Eve and, for his patience, was rewarded with wealth and a long life.

In Balla Koig on the Isle of Man, many elder trees had been cut down. That evening, the Feathag met. From miles around they came to do homage to the dead elder elves. The people in the neighbouring village heard the wind whistling through the grass and saw tiny lights on the hillside.

All that night the elves mourned for their murdered friends. So many elves came that there was scarcely room for them all. From south, from north, from east and from west, and from all the clans and tribes. They began to jostle one another. Soon words flew and swords were drawn. In the middle of their mourning, they began to fight. If any villagers had still been awake, they would have heard the wind roar, seen lights flashing and heard far-away cries. By dawn, the Fairies had vanished. Next to the chopped elder trees the townspeople found hundreds of elves' thumbs, reminders of their night-fought battle.

VODYANIYE

THE *Vodyany* has many things in common with the forest LESHY. Fiercely heathen, he will not use a deck of cards containing clubs because they remind him of the cross. Like the LESHY, he loves to drink, and is an inveterate gambler, often paying his debts with schools of fish. He can cause floods as easily as the LESHY can cause storms, and always does so when there is an underwater wedding and when he wakes in the spring, hungry and wild. He is more bloodthirsty than his forest relative, eating those who drown and storing their souls under jars in his underwater palace. There is one method of escape from the Vodyaniye but that is only open to young girls. If they drown, and especially if they commit suicide, they can choose to become RUSALKY, the companions of the Vodyaniye.

In his usual form, the Vodyany is singularly ugly. He doesn't wear clothes, is fat and has a bloated face. His old man's skin is pink and spongy, and he looks a little like a corpse. When he isn't drinking or carousing, he sits beside the river with a large club. He ties coloured ribbons to it and when curious children try to touch them, he beats them to death. In Bohemia, he appears on the surface of lakes as a clump of beautiful floating red flowers and drowns those who try to pick them.

Those most likely to be drowned by the Vodyany are those who bathe after dark without a cross around their necks. Men who carry a handful of dry earth or a piece of toasted bread are least likely to be caught.

Humans should not try to help a person who is drowning, or the Vodyany will be offended, and look for a new victim. When the Vodyany wakes in the spring, he should be appeased with offerings. Since he is most often seen near millstreams, the millers give him a black pig. Fishermen pour oil into the water for him. Those who keep bees throw the first swarm of the year into the millstream. But by far the most important gift for the Vodyany is the town offering. At the beginning of spring, a horse is bought and fattened for three days. It is then hog-tied and its head smeared with honey. Red ribbons are tied to the mane, two millstones are hung around the neck, and the animal is pushed at midnight through a hole in the ice to the waiting Vodyany.

Identification: The Vodyany appears as a fat naked old man with a large belly and a puffy face. When he changes into human form he can be recognized by the left tip of his shirt. It is always wet, and wherever the Vodyany sits down, he leaves a small puddle of water. His favourite fish form is that of a pike or a MER-MAN. In southern Slavic countries similar watermen are known as Vodni Mož, at the Italian–Yugoslavian border as Povoduji, and in Switzerland as Houggä-Ma.

A Vodyany

Habitat: The favourite home of the Vodyany is under mill-wheels and in millstreams. He can be encountered in rivers, springs, pools, streams or lakes – anywhere where there is running water. He is known from Yugoslavia to the eastern U.S.S.R.

A fisherman fishing one day in the lake came across a body floating in the water. He rowed closer, and thought he recognized a man from the village. The body was very heavy but he nevertheless loaded it into the boat and started home. He had rowed halfway across the lake when he heard loud laughter behind him.

Full of fear, he turned around and saw that the corpse was moving!

'Help! It's the end of the world! The dead are coming to life!'

The 'dead' Vodyany laughed at the fisherman. With one last guffaw, he jumped out of the boat.

A north Russian Vodyany had a large family and had to work very hard to feed them all. The neighbouring villagers understood his needs, but didn't relish the fact that he drowned *people* for his supper. After many discussions and town meetings, the villagers decided what they would do. For an entire month, not one person was to go near the lake and no animals were to drink there.

Finally the Vodyany surrendered. His family was starving. That night they decamped, never to be seen again.

unchetti

BAD dreams are caused by some elves. They come into bedrooms through keyholes and climb up on to sleepers' chests, cutting off their circulation and making it hard for them to breathe. This can prove fatal to old people. It is possible, however, to drive the elves away.

There are several methods that work against the Tuscan *Linchetto*. One is to place a large pan filled with birdseed on the sleeper's chest. The Linchetto will knock the pan over and spill the seed on the floor. Since he hates disorder, he will be forced to pick the seeds up, one by one. After that job, he won't be in any hurry to return! Another task that infuriates the Linchetto is trying to straighten a curly hair. But by far the most effective method is to make the Linchetto so disgusted that he won't want to return. His victim should turn on the light, get out of bed and go over to a chamber-pot placed in the other corner of the room. While sitting on the pot, he should take a big bite of cheese and bread and say, 'To shit with the Linchetto! I eat my bread and cheese and shit on his face!'* Disgusted, the Linchetto will depart.

The same method is effective against the Mazapegolo, but only if performed by a brown-haired girl.

The Linchetto does not only cause nightmares. He also spends much time in the barn, feeding his favourite animals and starving the ones he dislikes. He braids horses' manes, but these braids should never be undone. In them lie all the good qualities of the horse.

Identification: The Linchetto is variously classified as a NIGHT-ELF and as a FOLLETTO. He is said to have long ears, but is so rarely seen that this is hard to verify. He only appears at night and is usually invisible. He is reported to be about two feet high. He is also called Buffardello, Caccavecchia, and in Forlì Mazapegolo. The Mazapegolo is said to be slightly deformed.

Habitat: The Linchetto does not live in houses, but in the barn. He is found in Tuscany, in the vicinity of Lucca. The Mazapegolo lives only in Forlì.

A Lucchese boy had had several marriages annulled because as soon as he went to bed with his new bride, the Linchetto would begin to torment him, slapping and pinching him unmercifully. His wives thought him impotent and soon left.

However, one girl believed his story. When the Linchetto began to bother her husband, she sat straight up in bed. She asked the Linchetto to deliver a letter to India which she had forgotten to give to the postman. The elf vanished, only to reappear in a few minutes, as pesky as ever. The girl then sent him off to the Cape of Good Hope and to North and South America with three more letters, but he was so fast that the lovers only had time to sigh before he returned. Finally the exasperated girl gave the Linchetto a curly pubic hair and said, 'I want this to be straight, *completely straight*, by tomorrow morning.'

It was only later that they realized that the Linchetto hadn't bothered them for a long time.

'Well, is it straightened yet?' asked the girl.

The Linchetto's voice was so low it could hardly be heard. 'I can't do it.'

'But you *have* to do it by tomorrow morning!'

With a great howl of fear, the Linchetto threw away the hair and ran away from the house.

A brown-haired girl once tried to free herself from a Mazapegolo who was bothering her. She went to the chamber-pot with a sandwich in her hand. The Mazapegolo was so infuriated when he saw her sitting there that he shouted, 'You eat and piss and shit: you're a pig, a cow, an ugly whore!' Then he stalked out.

RUSALKY

As is the case with many spirits, the *Rusalky* are tied to a rigid schedule. Their activities, though, have been more carefully observed and better recorded than those of most elves.

The first time the Rusalky can be seen is on Holy Thursday. They surface in the water, or sit on the banks of streams and lakes, combing their long green hair. In the sixth week after Easter they move into the trees and beg pieces of linen from passers-by. This linen is then washed and carefully spread out to dry. Any human who steps on the Rusalky's wash will lose either his strength or his co-ordination.

During the seventh week after Easter, the Rusalky collect feathers and straw and build warm nests in their underwater palaces. Humans must not sew, wash linen or put up fences during this time and, if possible, not work at all. Those who do will probably lose their cattle and poultry. Humans meeting Rusalky in the woods should throw pieces of linen at them to keep them from doing harm. The Rusalky are offered garlands by young girls who hope that the water women will give them rich husbands in return.

On Sunday of the seventh week, a new phase begins in the life of the Rusalky. They then walk for the first time in the grain and hay fields, slipping invisibly through the stalks, singing, clapping their hands and making the grain wave in the wind. In most sections of the U.S.S.R., men chase them away, saying they are stealing the crops. These attempts are usually unsuccessful until 29 June.

Then the Rusalky begin a new activity: dancing. Each night they dance by the light of the moon and draw men into their circles. Those who have joined them never recover, but the grain grows better where they have danced. The Rusalky control the rain and wind that can increase or destroy a year's crop.

When the first snow falls in winter, the Rusalky vanish and are not seen again until the following spring. They hibernate in soft nests in the bottom of lakes and streams during this time.

Not only are the Rusalky tied to an iron schedule, but they are also watched over by the insanely jealous VODYANIYE. They can only go on land when the VODYANIYE allow it, and even then, must be sure to return on time.

Maybe because of the harshness of the life they lead, the Rusalky are often harsh with others. Those who can't answer their riddles are tickled to death. Those they catch in the woods without wormwood in their pockets suffer the same fate. They lure men into the water and then kill them, and those who bathe at night without a cross around their necks are drowned by the Rusalky or the VODYANIYE.

The Rusalky were originally girls who drowned, committed suicide, were strangled or were buried without a church funeral. After their death, such girls must be appeased with gifts of pancakes, alcohol and red eggs. If they do not get these offerings, they will haunt the forgetful relatives until the gifts are left for them.

Identification: The majority of Rusalky are very beautiful and have pale skin, white breasts, slender bodies, soft voices and beautiful long wavy hair. Their eyes are wild and they are naked. When they do wear clothes, they prefer long white unbelted dresses or coverings of green leaves. They cannot

A Rusalka

live if their hair dries out and always carry a comb with them. When it is pulled through their hair, it can cause a flood. These Rusalky live in the U.S.S.R. and in Romania.

The Rusalky near Saratov are much uglier and more gruesome than their relatives. They are always naked and their hair is dishevelled. They have fiery eyes, hunchbacks and sharp claws and love to drown humans.

Marine Rusalky are sometimes spoken of, but are so rare that very little is known of them.

Habitat: The real home of the Rusalky is in the water. When they come to land, they live in trees and among the grain. At the beginning of winter they return to the streams from which they take their names (in Russian, 'rus' means stream).

The Rusalky live in all of European Russia, in Romania and parts of Poland. In Bulgaria and Macedonia, similar water elves are called Judys.

A Rusalka married a Vodyany and they lived together in his underwater palace for many years.

The Rusalka did not think of her old life until one day she heard church bells. She went to the surface to see where the sound was coming from, and was overwhelmed by memories of trees and birds and the feeling of wind and sunlight. She wanted to go back to her village to visit family and friends. Without saying a word to her husband, she climbed out of the water and walked towards town.

But the town was not as she had imagined it. Not a soul recognized her. When she greeted them, they looked at her as if they hadn't seen her. That evening, broken-hearted, she returned to the Vodyany. Two days later the river roared in anger and her mutilated body was thrown upon the shore.

BROWNIES

THE best reward for a *Brownie* who has helped with the house-work is a bowl of cream and a hot-cake smeared with honey. In Scotland, the Brownie's craving for sweets is so well known that an especially delectable tidbit is known as 'a piece wad please a Brownie'.* Brownies also accept simpler offerings of beer and brown bread if these are left quietly in their favourite corner. Brownies hate any show of generosity and leave the house if the owner is rude enough to leave a suit of clothes for his naked helper.

If treated well, the Brownie can be an invaluable friend. Regularly fed and not ridiculed, he will milk the cows, churn the butter, mow hay, pasture the animals and even call a doctor if the mistress of the house is in labour. The Cornwall Browney is the bee guardian. The luck of the house depends on the Brownie. He makes everything run smoothly when he is happy, and ruins the family if he is miserable.

In Scotland, each house used to have its own Brownie who was especially helpful when the owners were brewing beer. They would pour a little malt from each batch into a holed stone called Brownie's stone, and he would hasten the brewing process and improve the flavour of the home brew. Increasing industrialization and the high taxes on malt later forced farmers to stop brewing, and many Brownies found them-selves without jobs. They can still be found in remote English and Scottish villages, but are seen less frequently than before.

Identification: About twenty inches high, they are often invisible. When they can be seen, they have shaggy brown hair which covers them from head to foot. They have wrinkled old faces and brown skin. They are naked or wear old tattered clothes of coarse brown wool. The Scottish Lowland Brownies have no real noses, just two nostrils, and the Highland Brownies have no fingers or toes. An interesting Lowland Brownie is the Wag at the Wa', an old teetotaller with crooked legs and a long tail. He lives on the pothook in the fireplace and always has a toothache. The Bodachan Sabhaill are Highland barn Brownies.

Habitat: Brownies live in the British Isles in Cornwall, northern England, Scotland, Orkney and Shetland, and have even been seen in Ireland. Their Welsh relatives are called BWCIOD. They usually live in human houses but also stay in caves, hollow trees, rocks or river banks near houses.

Most Brownie stories tell how the Brownie is 'laid'. A gift of new clothes will lay him – force him to leave a house forever.

The Cauld Lad of Hilton was an English Brownie who helped in the kitchen of Hilton Hall. He cleaned everything up if the kitchen had been left dirty. But if the plates had been washed and stacked, he would hurl them around the room. The servants soon caught on to his ways and went to bed without cleaning anything up. In the morning, the kitchen was spotless.

One day, a maid overheard the Cauld Lad complaining:

> 'Wae's me, wae's me!
> The acorn's not yet
> Fallen from the tree
> That's to grow the wood
> That's to make the cradle
> That's to grow the bairn
> That's to grow to a man
> That's to lay me.'

A Brownie

The maids didn't like to see the Brownie unhappy. They made him a green cloak and hood and put them in his corner, little knowing that their gift would lay him. He was overjoyed with the gift and danced round and round, admiring himself in his new clothes. That night he vanished, never to return. The women had, in fact, been able to lay him where no man could.

A Berwickshire Brownie had faithfully mowed and threshed the corn for years until someone criticized his work. This angered him so much that he carted all the corn a distance of two miles and threw it over Raven's Crag.

'It's no' weel mowed! It's no' weel mowed! – Then it's ne'er be mowed by me again; I'll scatter it ow'r the Raven Stane, and they'll hae some wark ere it's mowed again!'

He never returned to the farm, nor was he ever seen again in Scotland.

Another mischievous Brownie placed himself between two serving girls who were sharing a piece of stolen cake and took it from them, bite by bite. They couldn't see Brownie, so each thought the other had stolen her cake. The maids had begun to hit each other and swear when suddenly the Brownie laughed, 'Ha, ha, ha, Brownie has't a'!'

BWCA

THE Welsh *Bwca* or Bwbach is a close relative of the BROWNIE. If humoured and treated with respect, he can be very helpful.

He churns the butter if the kitchen and the fireplace have been swept and a bowl of cream set out next to the newly lighted fire. But if mistreated or insulted in any way, Bwca will lose his temper and refuse to work. He does not easily forget humiliation and revenges himself with frightening violence. He bangs on the walls, throws things, pinches sleepers, tosses people through the air, destroys clothes, rips holes in wool, tells everyone's innermost secrets out loud, howls, screeches. and even beats his tormentors. If at this point the Bwca will not abandon the house on his own, it is best to force him to leave, for he will never regain his earlier good humour. Care should be taken to protect oneself with iron, holy water or crosses made from mountain ash. Then a wise man should be called in who is an expert at Bwca-banishing.

Identification: The Bwciod are about the same size as BROWNIES. Often invisible, they are very good at hiding and are virtually impossible to find unless they decide to show themselves. They have dark skin and dress in coarse Welsh farmers' clothes. Most have long noses.

Habitat: They live in Wales and only frequent houses where they are well fed and well treated. They despise teetotallers. Occasionally they live in fields or caves next to the house, but are most often found near the warmth of the fireplace.

A Bwca had become the special friend of a serving girl and used to help her with the chores around the house. She in return would leave the Bwca a bowl of milk and some bread every night. But once she decided to make fun of the Bwca, forgetting that he had very little sense of humour. She left urine in place of his milk and went to bed, laughing to herself.

Bwca was not at all amused. In fact, he was angry.

'The idea that the thick-buttocked lass should give barley

bread and piss to the Bwca!' he grumbled. He grabbed the girl by the neck, dragged her out of bed, and beat and kicked her through the house until he heard the menservants coming. Then he ran away.

His next home was a nearby farm, but the girl there was just as impolite and managed to discover his real name. She made sounds of leaving the house, but actually stayed indoors to spy on the Bwca. Soon he began to sing. 'How she would laugh, did she know that Gwaryn-a-Throt is my name!' When he discovered that she *did* know his name, he left in a huff, swearing he would never trust women again.

At his next home he made friends with the master of the house. All went well until the man was called to war. In his loneliness Bwca tried to amuse himself, banging on the walls and teasing the men at their ploughing. When his pranks stopped being playful, the household lost all patience with him. They called in a wise man who seized the Bwca by his long nose and banished him to the Red Sea.

SKOGSRÅ OR WOOD TROLLS

IN SWEDEN during the seventeenth century, many death warrants were issued in which the cause of death was listed as 'involvement with a Skogsnufva'. Many of these involvements were sexual, but even non-sexual relationships with Wood Women were thought dangerous enough to lead to death.

Even today, great care should be taken in dealing with the *Skogsrå* or *Wood Trolls*. The first thing to be remembered is that, despite their gentle appearance, the Skogsnufvar, the female Skogsrå, are not without means of defence. Not only are their husbands willing to come to their aid, but the women

A Bwca

can also gain control over men, and madden, sicken or kill
them. If they can make a man answer, 'Yes,' to one of their
calls in the woods, he is in their power. They lead him astray
for hours, forcing him through brambles and thorns, enticing
him into bogs, watching him peel off his soaking clothes and
then, with demoniacal laughter, tumbling him cold and shivering on to dry land. If a man refuses to answer one of their calls,
they can trap him in huge invisible nets from which he can
only free himself at the sound of a church bell.

But the Skogsnufva only gains complete control over a man
once she has slept with him. No matter how hard he then tries,
he will not be able to forget her and will sicken and die from
longing. Some exceptional men do not sicken immediately
but fall prey to loneliness, melancholy and madness, all because
of their night with the Skogsnufva. Children born of these
unions are either monstrous abortions who are later changed for
healthy human children, or humans possessed with elfin powers.

Although the Skogsnufva and her husband the Skovmann
seem very dangerous, disaster can be avoided by a few simple
precautions. Travellers should never answer, 'Yes,' to any
sounds heard in the forest, but should always call out, 'He!'
Those who feel they are being led astray should immediately
turn their coats or socks inside out and say the paternoster
backwards. Garlic and steel also work effectively against the
Skogsrå. Hunters should always leave a few coins or a little
food on a tree-stump before entering the forest, and if possible
should enter into a compact with the Skogsnufva over hunting
rights. Otherwise they might inadvertently wound one of the
Wood Woman's animals. When someone is in mortal danger,
offensive action can be taken against the Skogsnufva, although
there is the hazard that bad luck will then follow the aggressor.
The Skogsnufvar are mortally afraid of thunder, wolves and
the Wild Hunt,[1] and can be wounded with one of their own
hairs fired from a shotgun.

[1] The Wild Hunt is a train of elfin or giant beings, raging through the
landscape with force and violence, giving rise to storms and winds,

Identification: The Skogsrå are Wood Folk or Wood Trolls; the Skougman, Skogsråt, Skovmann or Hulte are Wood Men; and the Skogsjungfru or Skogsnufvar Wood Women.

The males are shape-changers, like most forest sprites, and can expand or shrink at will. Their true form is that of old men with wide hats, although they appear as horned owls or come riding a storm or whirlwind. Their height varies from human size to that of the tallest tree in the forest. They can easily be recognized when in human form by the long cow tail which they try to hide behind them.

The Skogsnufvar are at first glance beautiful, seductive creatures with sweet voices, long breasts and flowing hair. At second glance it can be seen that they have claws in the place of fingernails and that they always keep their backs hidden. Anyone who manages to catch a glimpse of their backs will see either a long cow tail trailing out from under their furs or will notice that they have no back: what should be solid flesh is instead a transparent hollow. All Skogsnufvar can change shapes, assuming any natural forms they wish.

The Lundjungfrur are Skogsnufvar who live in trees near houses and prefer to remain invisible to humans. The Puu-Halijad are male Estonian tree sprites who live in groves of trees behind houses, like the Latvian Mahjas Kungs.

Habitat: The Skogsrå are wood and forest sprites. They can't travel far from the confines of their forest and their lives are tied to those of their native trees. They punish humans who harm them in any way. Primarily Swedish elves, they have also been seen along the Baltic coast.

---

uprooting trees and spreading destruction in its path. The Wilde Männer are most often associated with the Wild Hunt, choosing the weakest and gentlest members of the forest community as their quarry.

Twilight was fading into evening and, even in the forest, the stars could be seen. A charcoal burner sat beside his fire in a clearing, tired from a day's hard work. Suddenly the figure of a woman materialized beside him. It was a Skogsnufva.

The charcoal burner had heard stories of these women, of how they seduced men and then drove them mad with desire, or how they led them astray in the underbrush and then laughed at them. In his mind, any Skogsnufva was by definition a she-devil, a sorceress and a temptress all in one. The one standing before him had obviously come to harm him, and must be driven away. The man picked up a burning stick from his fire and threw it at the Skogsnufva. The sparks hit her skirt and it burst into flames.

The Wood Woman, with a look of disdain, turned her back on him, and called loudly to her mate, the Skovmann. Within a fraction of a second, a great wind rose and blew into the clearing, extinguishing the flames. The Skogsnufva vanished but the wind remained, rattling every leaf in the forest and roaring vengeance. The charcoal burner was forced to seek shelter and wait there until the fury of the Skovmann subsided.

'When I was young and foolish, I married a human and he taught me what I know of mortal ways. We spent many nights together, and I soon became a mother. One day, he went back from the forest to fetch our meal. I made him promise to hit the tree on the right side of the path three times on his return. He promised but then forgot, and came unannounced. It was then that he saw me as I am: a naked Wood Woman with a cow tuft on her tail.

'He turned around, went back to the tree and gave it three good knocks. As he came again into the clearing, I met him, his loving wife, dressed in skirt and blouse, and without a tail.

'Mortal men are vain, and can't feel the sap in the trees, or the blood flowing in their veins. I, who had been closer to him than any human, suddenly became a monster in his eyes. He had loved me, but his love turned to hate, all because of a forgotten promise and a glimpse of a cow's tail.

'One winter's day he led me and his children out on to the middle of a frozen lake and abandoned us. I called to him to return and take us with him, but his feet did not hesitate. The wind was cold, but his heart was colder. Night fell and I heard the wolves. I hurried with the children to escape but the wolves were already there, their eyes glittering like snapping glass. They saw us unprotected, without fire, and circled slowly round us, howling.

'Only then did I remember my sister, almost forgotten in long years spent in bed and kitchen.

' "Little one," I called to her, "who rides the wind, hear me if you can, and help us, for the wolves are here!"

'Almost without hope, I waited for her to come. The wolves took the little ones first and soon I was left alone. Then my sister flew down, cradled me in her arms, and took me away on the back of the wind. For days I stayed with her, sick and hoping to die. But I did not die, and lived to tell my tale.

'My sister went to find my husband. She followed him for weeks without touching him, fearing the amulet he had hung around his neck. One day, though, he took it off to bathe. My sister saw her chance and, sweeping down upon him, broke his neck.

'Mortal men are vain, and can't feel the sap in the trees, or the blood flowing in their veins. But if you can hear me and have listened to my song, remember the Wood Woman who trusted a man.'

KORNBÖCKE

and hausböcke

MOST northern house sprites are descendants of tree or wood spirits. The *Hausböcke* are close relatives of field spirits. These field spirits, or field-goats, are called *Kornböcke* and correspond to the Greek and Italian goat people.

The corn and grain Böcke live in the fields, make the grain ripen and ride the breezes that ripple the stalks. They scare and punish children who come to pick blue cornflowers. The Böcke are either killed or are forced into hibernation when the fields are harvested. The reapers then chase them through the grain with their sickles until there is only one sheaf left standing. If this sheaf is cut, the goat hidden in it will die. If it is left, he will use it as food until his winter hibernation.

The field-goats were originally brought into the house on the shortest day of the year, in long processions. Today, it is no longer necessary to bring them into the house: they come of their own accord. The Scandinavian Julbuk lives in the woods during the summer, in the fields in autumn and then inches closer to the house, day by day, until 23 December when he comes indoors. If he is plentifully fed, he will leave promptly without doing any mischief. If he finds his reception lacking in any way, he will spill the beer in the cellar, throw weevils into the flour and make the grain rot. Knecht Ruprecht, a German Hausbock, also comes indoors at Christmas time walking in a procession with two other figures, wearing fur or straw and carrying a long pole adorned with a goat's skin and wooden goat's head with horribly clacking jaws. In recent years he has been so confused with St Nicholas that the two are now very difficult to tell apart.

Because the field-goats are so irascible, they have been used by mothers to scare disobedient children for many hundreds of years. The Irish Phooka and the German Jüdel and Klaubauf have all been accused of the most heinous crimes, from child-molesting to kidnapping and even murder.

Identification: The Kornbock is so often invisible that it is difficult to give a good description of him. His size changes with the height of the grain in the field. He presents himself to humans in various forms, as a goat, a bird, a cat, a wolf or even an insect, and has as many names as disguises. Most of the time he hides in the fields as a cornflower. The Scottish Urisk and the Yugoslavian Čatez are field sprites who have a man's head and shoulders and the lower body of a goat.

The Hausböcke have many names. The Scandinavian Julbuk or Jolabukkar have horns and always wear furs. The German Knecht Ruprecht dresses in shaggy clothing or wraps himself in furs and straw. He carries a large sack filled with ashes and has a staff, called the 'Klapperbock', which is covered with a goat's skin and is topped by a wooden goat's head. Ruprecht has a long beard. The Klaubauf has horns, a long beard, long fingers and a long nose. He carries a sack and dresses in furs. Although usually quiet, he gnashes his teeth and roars loudly when angered. The Irish Phooka likes to appear as a goat, a pig or a horse.

Habitat: The Kornböcke and Hausböcke live in northern and eastern Europe. The Kornböcke, Čatez and Urisks live in grain fields, in light woods and near waterfalls. The Julbuk lives in the woods during the summer and the fields in the autumn, like Knecht Ruprecht and Klaubauf. The Phooka spends most of his time inside the house, like the Scandinavian Husbuk.

MOERAE

IN ANCIENT Greece, the three Fates or *Moerae* determined the destiny of each new-born child. Ancient mythologists elevated them to the position of half-goddesses, representing them as three distinct individuals, Clotho, Lachesis and Atropos. One spun the thread of life, one wound it and one cut it short.

In popular belief, their duties are not so clearly defined. Each region or valley knows its own tales of the three spinning, fortune-telling women. They are disfigured from their work: some are crooked from bending over the wheel, some have hideous drooping eyelids from working so late at night, others have pendulous lips from twisting the thread. Another has an enormous bottom from perpetually sitting, and still another long teeth from breaking the thread.

As the personifications of change, the Moerae appear at the three most important moments in a man's life: at his birth, his marriage and his death.

Their first appearance is on the third night after a baby's birth when they come to foretell his future, give advice and favour him with his birthmarks. Great care should be taken to prepare the house for their arrival. It should be well swept and a table should be neatly laid out with honey, bread and three white almonds. In certain areas of Greece, water, coins and precious gifts are also placed beside the food. The door should be left open, a light kept burning, and the house should be very quiet. Once the Moerae have pronounced the child's fate, it cannot be changed.

Girls who want to marry and women about to give birth seek the help of the Moerae. They make pilgrimages to their caves and leave them offerings of cakes and honey. The Moerae are also invited to weddings, at which honey-covered almonds are distributed to the guests.

One of the Moerae

The Moerae appear for the last time at a person's death, when they come to usher him out of our world.

The ancient Romans knew the Moerae under the name of Parcae but, like many other Greek imports, they did not thrive in Italy. Nevertheless, other descendants of the Moerae still live there. They are the three FATE who come at Epiphany bringing gifts and punishing naughty children: the Befana, the Maratega and the Rododesa.

Identification: The spinning women range in size from three to five feet. They are extremely old, often very ugly or disfigured. Their clothing consists of the dark dresses and shawls usually worn by old women. The Maratega is ancient and brittle and can stretch to incredible heights, while the Rododesa has the power of changing her fingers and hands into sweets which she then gives to children.

The Befana is the most famous of the three, appearing throughout Italy as a little old woman who climbs down the chimney or slips through the door to leave sweets for good children and coal for bad ones. She can only be seen on this one night in January, for she spins the rest of the year, hidden in the chimney or in some dark cave.

Habitat: The Moerae live in dark caves in Greece, Rhodes, Romania and Albania. The Albanian Fates are also called the Wives of Rica, while the Albanians in Athens call them the Miri. The Befana lives in dark caves or in the chimney and is known throughout Italy. Similar spinning women are known under the name of Metten, Parzae or Nornen in northern Europe; Witte Wijven in Holland; Trois Maries in Switzerland; Urd, Skulld or Verdandi in Scandinavia; Bonnes Dames in France and Rojenice in Friuli and Yugoslavia. They occur under many names in other sections of Europe but are so often confused with the local nature and fertility spirits that the name often does not apply to them alone.

A girl had a year in which to prepare her trousseau, but she was lazy and didn't finish it in time. Three women appeared to help her on the condition that she invite them to the wedding. The first was named Nose: her nose reached to her feet, the result of a lifetime of weaving. The second was named Lip: her lip hung to the floor because she had spent her life sewing. The third was called Bottom and was as broad as a cow, from a lifetime spent in a chair knitting. The three women set to work and quickly finished the girl's dowry.

On the wedding day, the first guests to arrive were the three old women. When the bridegroom saw their ugliness, and recognized it as a consequence of a lifetime of weaving, sewing and knitting, he forbade his wife ever to touch a loom or needle again. She happily obeyed.

T he midwife, peeping in through the keyhole, saw three beautiful white women bending over the newly born child.

'I decree that he will become a great priest,' said the first.

'No, he will have a harder lot, and die as a soldier,' contradicted the second.

'This child won't even grow to be a man,' said the third. 'On his eighteenth birthday, he will be struck by lightning and die. *That* will be his fate.'

The midwife was very worried by the prophecy of the Rojenice and at the first opportunity told the child's mother. The mother was a wealthy lady, and decided that no cost would be spared to save her only son. She built a great fort for him, surrounded it with nine massive walls and closed him inside it a few days before his eighteenth birthday.

The sky was already dark when the day dawned, and by noon a storm was raging. A bolt of lightning hit the loft next to the house and started a fire. There was no escape for the boy through the nine locked gates. He was burned on his birthday, as foretold by the Rojenice.

ouenoe

THE *Duende* are unique among elves in that they cling so closely to their chosen homes. They cannot be exorcized, and, like the FOLLETS, have no fear of priests and holy water. They can only be forced to leave a house when the inhabitants move, taking with them all that makes it 'home' for the Duende.

The Duende are NIGHT-ELVES, vanishing long before the first rays of light brighten the morning sky. It is at night that they play their endless pranks, scaring the fearful and causing the brave to lose much sleep. The most mischievous Duende think up no end of practical jokes to amuse themselves. One of their most famous games is called Nip the Napper, in which they dream up new ways to wake sleepers: by breathing down their necks, tickling them with icy fingers, pulling off the covers or stroking them with cold hands. They also move the furniture around, throw stones and clay at the roof, hurl plates out of the windows, rattle chains, sing, dance, or use the sleeping humans as horses. Despite their obvious delight in such games, many Duende also work during the night in return for a bowl of milk. They clean the house, light new fires and do repairing jobs and light smith work.

Identification: The Duende are around two feet high, and have the ability to make themselves invisible or to change shape. When in their normal form, they dress in green, red, or grey, and always wear a small hat. In most cases the hat is red, although some Duende prefer dark hoods.

One of the Duende

Habitat: The Duende are universally known in Spain and Portugal. They live almost exclusively indoors, preferring isolated and abandoned buildings far from the bustle of city life. They have been seen in deserted towers as well as in caves and ruins.

seligen
frxulein

'THE world has changed, but not for the better. The Wilde Männer have come into the land, and driven away the Seligen.'* According to Tirolean farmers, it has become harder to farm the land and the soil itself has become less fruitful since the *Seligen* went away. They were chased away by their enemies the 'Wild Men' or Wilde Männer.

The Wilde Männer are storm-causing giants who are overtaken by a destructive fury early each spring. They then roar through the forest, uprooting trees and plants and hunting the meekest of all the wood spirits: the Seligen, the AGUANE and the Moosweibchen. The Seligen are only safe from the Wilde Männer if they can find a tree-stump with three crosses cut on it. Once on such a stump, the Wild Men have no more power over the Seligen and must give up the chase.

Most Seligen have disappeared but there are still a few who make occasional appearances on Earth. These should be treated with great respect by humans, because they are among the most benevolent female elves. Men who cut crosses on tree-stumps before the tree touches the ground or who in any way help the Seligen are richly rewarded.

When they are not threatened by the Wilde Männer, the Seligen Fräulein care for the woods and animals of which they are the mistresses. They fiercely protect chamois and deer from hunters, and milk them in underground stalls. They make the hay and flax grow faster and often lend a hand when the farmers are harvesting. They help with the milking and herding, spinning and weaving. They teach their favourites the art of herb-healing and rescue lost travellers.

Despite their willingness to work, the Seligen can be driven away if their hair is touched by a man, if anyone curses in their presence, if they are hit in anger, if they are called by their proper names or if they are given gifts of clothing. Sometimes they are called away from a house by a voice which tells them of a death in the family.

Identification: The Dialen, Dive, Seligen Fräulein and Schneefräulein are all Wilden Fräulein. They are closely related to the male Waldzwergen, NORGGEN and Lörggen, and often mate with them.

The Wilden Fräulein dress in shimmering iridescent white clothes and have long blonde hair and bright blue eyes. About five feet tall, they can be told from humans only by their extraordinary beauty. They are always slender, and often barefoot. The Seligen love bells of every sort, and are fond of dancing. The Dialen have goat's feet. The Schneefräulein dress in white and wear crystal jewellery.

Habitat: The large Wilde Frauen are known throughout Germany and Austria, the smaller Wilden Fräulein only in southern Germany and the Tirol. The Seligen are native to the Tirol, the Dialen live in Unterengadin on the Austrian–Swiss border, the Schneefräulein are from the Austrian Stubeital and the Dive from the Italian Tirol. The Swiss Frohn also belong to the same family.

The Wilden Fräulein live for the most part underground, or in mountain caves. They frequently stay with humans in their houses. The Schneefräulein live in larch and beech forests.

During haying, a girl came to a farmer and offered to help him with the cutting. Because she was such a beautiful young girl he was more than happy to take her on. When he discovered what a good worker she was, he was even happier. What he could usually cut in several days, with her help he could now cut in just one day.

The farmer was so impressed with her that he began to think about marriage. Such a worker would certainly make him a good wife. But the girl refused his offers and said she must leave as soon as the haying was done. Each day the farmer liked her more and wanted less to let her go.

As the last section of hay was being mowed, the man decided to make the girl stay. Just as she was binding the last sheaf, he caught her left foot and tied her fast. She still wouldn't give in to his demands. She struggled until she freed herself, breaking her leg. Crying with pain, the elf woman vanished from sight.

Because of his greed, the farmer never saw the girl again. A few days later he fell and broke his own left leg. The bone never set properly, and he had a limp to his dying day.

A bold young man was out hunting chamois and got lost high in the mountains. Tired from walking and from lack of food, he slipped and fell. Several hours later three Seligen found him lying there unconscious. They carried him to their underground palace and for three days he was pampered and healed by the most beautiful women he had ever seen. Then his idyll came to an end, and the Seligen told him he must leave.

'Is there no way for me to come back? Won't I ever see you again?' the young man asked.

The Seligen were firm. 'Only on the condition that you promise never to hunt another of our animals and never to tell anyone that you have been here or let them follow you here, and that you never give your love to another woman. If you keep your promise, you can visit us for three days during each full moon.'

The boy gave his word and it seemed a small price to pay to see the beautiful Seligen again.

The boy returned to his village and to his old life but refused to join any of his friends on their hunting trips. At the next full moon he disappeared for three days. When he returned, he was moody and depressed. His mother asked where he had been but he refused to answer.

Each month he returned to the Seligen, and each month he grew more and more melancholy. His mother was alarmed, and one day decided to follow him. As she came to the opening that led to the Seligen's underground garden and discovered her son's secret, a landslide rolled down from the top of the mountain and sealed the door.

The boy knew that he would never see the Seligen again. For a long time, he didn't leave his room and wouldn't speak to anyone, until one day a friend persuaded him to go hunting. Once out in the fresh air, the boy's old love of the hunt returned. A chamois crossed his path and he galloped madly off after it. The goat led him through woods and over hills. He left his companions behind and followed the animal on foot. Then the chamois stopped and he shot at it. A strange light spread out from where the chamois was standing and, shimmering with blinding brightness, formed itself into three women's bodies. Dazzled by their beauty, the boy took a step backwards as the Seligen walked toward him. He now remembered his promise, but it was too late: his foot caught on the edge of the cliff and he tumbled over, the vision of the angry Seligen blinding him.

The Wild Hunt[1] was once racing through the forest. A shepherd heard a savage howl as the hunt passed by and caught a glimpse of something white between the trees. He thought it was a Selige and laughed to himself because he knew there were no crossed stumps in the forest.

'Hey, you old goat! Have a great time hunting, and bring me a piece tomorrow!' he called out.

The Wild Man didn't answer, and the shepherd laughed at his joke.

The next morning he got his answer. On the door of his hut he found a part of the Wild Man's catch: a piece of a Selige was nailed there, dripping blood. The forest trembled with a howl. Terrified, the shepherd grabbed his axe, and quickly chopped down a fir tree, hacking three crosses in the stump. As he made the last cut, a storm broke loose and drove him back to his hut. The bloody carcass was gone from his door, but its memory remained vivid in his mind.

A Selige had been captured by Jordan, a Wild Man, and had to serve his wife, the Fangga. The Selige worked hard in the house but never could bring herself to like its owners. Her only friend was a large black cat, also a servant of the Fangga.

One day the Selige was left alone in the house. She took advantage of the opportunity and fled. She ran until she came to a house on the outskirts of a village and there offered her services. She was taken on as a maid and the cat that had followed her was given a place by the fire. In no time at all, thanks to her untiring efforts, her master became one of the richest men in the valley.

One day a friend of her master's was on his way to town with some oxen and heard a voice calling from the woods.

[1] See note on p. 200.

'Oxen-man! Oxen-man! Tell Hitte-Hatte she should go home! Jordan is dead!'

The man stopped at his friend's house on the way home, and told the story of the voice in the forest. Hitte-Hatte dropped her spoon and cried, 'If Jordan's dead, then I'm happy! Take care of the hairy house-worm [the cat], take my thanks, and have good luck with the cattle. If you'd asked me more I would have told you more.' With those words the Selige vanished and was not seen again.

FOLLETS

ALTHOUGH the names *Follet,* LUTIN and FÉE are often used interchangeably, the elves they represent belong to quite different groups.

The name Follet is used primarily for the descendants of elves who lived in the once-bustling underground dolmen metropolises. As these elf cities lost their strength and power, the Follets moved away and came more and more under the influence of human beings.

Perhaps because of their long association with humans, the Follets cannot be driven away by exorcisms or holy water but continue their pranks right under the nose of Church and priest. There is little that the Follets hold sacred, for they are a merry, independent group and know no masters. They love to bother women who are spinning, and rub the cattle so hard with straw that scabs form on their hides. They pelt houses with stones, sticks and kitchen crockery. They are not beyond making crude practical jokes, like the Farfadet who took down his breeches in front of three old women spinning in front of the fire and then vanished laughing up the chimney. The only thing they fear is steel, and a good strong knife often drives them away.

Like many practical jokers, the Follets can be brought to heel, and changed into relatively helpful workers. Humans who have the patience to withstand their high jinks and who do not give way to anger and retribution earn the respect of these Little People. As proof of friendship, the Follets bring presents, complete unfinished work, and feed and pasture the animals.

Identification: The first descriptions of house Follets tell of little men dressed like medieval jesters, with bright multi-coloured coats covered with tiny bells. The present-day Far-fadets are rarely seen but, when visible, always wear red coats and breeches. The cave Follets are between one and two feet high, hairy, with long beards and hair and dark skin. They usually wear swords, so small that they can double as corsage pins. When the Follets take animal form, it is usually as goats.

Habitat: The Follets can be seen throughout France, in French Switzerland, in Belgium, in Corsica and in Mallorca. They live in underground caves, in sea or land caverns, or among dunes. Those who live with humans come into the house through the chimney or the cat-hole.

A Mallorcan miller's wife was once approached by a group of tiny Dimonis-Boyets who begged her to give them a little wheat.

'Give *you* grain? Why, you've probably stolen half a bushel already! But if you really want it,' the woman told them, 'you can wash this wool. When it's completely white, come back and I'll give you the grain.'

The Boyets looked at the wool and then back at the woman. Some of the smaller elves started to cry.

'But this wool is black! We'll never be able to make it white!'

A Follet

The miller's wife just laughed at them. She had asked them a favour and knew that they were forced to do her bidding.

Very slowly and very sadly, the Dimonis-Boyets left the mill, and were never seen again on the island. Some day they will return with a skein of bleached white wool, and expect their grain.

FOUNTAIN WOMEN

THE Korrigans and female Lamignak are the special guardians of springs and fountains. They make their homes in underground caverns but spend most of their waking hours next to their springs. In the case of the Korrigans, these springs and fountains are usually found near dolmens and standing stones. The elves rarely awaken before sundown.

The French *Fountain Women* are at their most beautiful at night, when the moonlight transforms them into awesome diaphanous figures. It is then that they hold secret rituals which change the springs into healing waters. When the moon is at its fullest, they comb their long hair with golden combs, as slowly and as patiently as the waters fall from their fountains. They sing old songs in voices so sweet that the night stops to listen to them. When their hair has been carefully brushed, the Korrigans and Lamignak bathe in the cool water, still singing their songs. It is not particularly dangerous for human women to look on while they are bathing, but it is hazardous for males. The man who catches the Korrigan at her bathing must pay with his body. He is bound to marry her within three days, or die.

It has been said that the Korrigans are the grand-daughters of the nine holy druidesses of ancient Gaul, but it is more likely that both are descendants of the KORRED, the Dark Elves who live under Brittany's dolmens. The Korrigans have, in time, through their association with water, become more and more ethereal until they can now be rightfully classified as Dusky Elves. They still retain their pagan beliefs to such an extent that the sight of a priest's cassock will send them into a rage and the name of the Virgin Mary is odious to their ears. Every spring, they hold a festival at which they drink the secret of poetry and of earthly wisdom from a crystal goblet. The man audacious enough to interrupt this festival will pay for it with his life.

The Lamignak are less violently anti-Catholic than the Korrigans, but cannot divorce themselves from the old ways. Although the two species can understand each other perfectly, they cannot be understood by humans. They say exactly the reverse of what we would say. If a Lamignak remarks that it will be a nice day, this means that it will rain or snow. If she prophesies bad weather, it will undoubtedly be the nicest week of the year.

Identification: The Korrigans, as well as the Lamignak, are two feet tall and have well-proportioned bodies. They always dress in flowing white clothes and their hair is long and blonde. They can both change shapes, appearing as spiders, eels or snakes. At night, the Korrigans display extraordinary beauty and their golden hair shines with an inner light. But during the day their hair whitens, their eyes turn red and their skin wrinkles like that of old, old women.

Not all Lamignak are fountain elves. Many, both male and female, live deep in the mountains, in caves, woods and caverns. They have the same relationship to the fountain Lamignak as the KORRED to the Korrigans, and are darker in colouring and shorter in stature than the Fountain Women.

Habitat: The Korrigans can be found in Brittany, the Lamignak in the Basque Pyrenees. They live almost exclusively in the vicinity of springs, fountains and water sources. The Korrigans do not usually appear above ground in the daytime, and both they and the Lamignak make their homes in richly decorated subterranean grottoes.

Lord Nann had married young and his wife was pregnant. When she gave birth to twins he went out into the forest to hunt a deer to give her as a present. Instead of a buck, he found a white doe and followed it until evening.

He then stopped to drink at a stream that belonged to a Korrigan who was combing her hair with a golden comb on the bank.

'How dare you muddy the water!' she cried. 'If you don't marry me, you will waste away for seven years, or die in three days.'

'I can't marry you,' answered Lord Nann, 'for I've been married a year already. And as for dying – I'll do that when God commands it.'

Lord Nann rode back to the castle and, in spite of his disbelief, soon fell sick. In three days he died but no one dared to break the news to his wife. On her way to church, she passed by a new grave and discovered the truth. Because of her grief and the Korrigan's magic, within a few days she was also dead.

POLTERSPRITES

EVERYONE has heard of Poltergeists, but few know that most 'poltering' or knocking sounds are not attributable to occultists' 'spirits' but to a specific class of home sprites called *Poltersprites*. They are descendants of KOBOLDE and are, like

A Poltersprite

them, shape-changers. They help with the housework and do various jobs on the farm, but their chief delight is in making noise. They travel around the house in the shape of squirrels or cats, rattling and knocking enough to shake the dishes in the cupboard and to make the silverware vibrate on the table. They throw nuts down cellar stairs, thump softly under the wainscoting, patter overhead, throw rocks at the roof, make the beds squeak, and swing on creaky doors. When someone in the family is about to die, their clattering is even louder, warning of the coming event.

Identification: Poltersprites, though descendants of KO-BOLDE, are not bound to trees or to figurines but are free to travel as they wish. They wear rough clothes of green or grey and have red or grey caps called 'Tarnkappen' which give them the power of invisibility.

In France, the Sotret is a well-known Poltersprite. In England, Knocky Boh is famous. Some German sprites are called Ekerken, Klopferle, Poppele, Pulter Klaes and Nick-Nocker. In eastern Europe, they go by the names of Bildukka, Ztrazhnik, Bubak, Strashila and Straszydlo.

Habitat: The Poltersprites live primarily indoors and are known in most of Europe.

A Swiss Poltersprite once drove a family to madness with his continual pounding and racketing. They sent for the village priest to drive the obnoxious sprite away but even he could do nothing. The second time the priest came, he was able to ban the sprite into a hole in the wall, but only on the condition that the owners of the house give him an offering of oil for the church every year.

The house was quiet for ten years, and the family gave the

priest the oil regularly. The tenth year they forgot and, since then, the sprite has poltered without interruption.

VILY

AN OLD Slavonic saying is, 'Whether the Vila is white or black, she will always be a bad Vila.'* In other words, the only good *Vila* is no Vila at all. They are held to be even more malicious, jealous and wicked than their relatives the Greek NEREIDES. Men are cruel to them, and they in turn are cruel to men.

The exclusively female Vily live mainly in mountain forests and on craggy peaks. They protect and care for the springs, streams, trees, plants and animals within their domains. At times, their possessiveness becomes pathological. They go to absurd lengths to keep intruders away from their trees and their woods, even poisoning streams so that no man will drink there. They speak the speech of animals, and herd chamois and deer. Any hunter who is foolish enough to shoot one of their animals will be punished with mutilation, blindness, dumbness or death.

When men come into Vila territory, the Vily often shout so loudly that the men are sickened with fright. Those who stay too long in their lands are shot with arrows, die suddenly of a heart attack, sunstroke or lumbago, or are buried under avalanches.

Beautiful women should be particularly careful not to go near Vila-woods for even the best-disposed and kindest Vily are subject to fits of jealousy. They do not like to see beauty in any other women.

It is said that Vily are only born during a fine rain on those summer days when the sunlight breaks into tiny rainbows on the tree branches. Their nature is like their birth weather, at times cloudy, at times sunny. Despite their jealous and malicious tendencies, most Vily also have a positive side. Because they can cause sicknesses, they can also cure them, and know the healing properties of each and every plant under their protection. They cure the mentally ill, give planting advice, bring the dead back to life and show where treasures are hidden.

Children they take under their protection are always well cared for, as are the fields, streams, woods, and animals of which they are the mistresses. They befriend brave and fearless men and change themselves into horses so that their heroes won't have to travel on foot. They marry young men, although their insatiability and jealous tempers often make difficulties.

The most desirable relationship to have with a Vila is to become her blood-sister. Those who have been struck with Vila arrows or have been taken by the Vily often join with them in elective sisterhood, and are allowed to return to Earth after a period of three, seven, thirteen or twenty-one years. They are called Vileniki or Vilenaci and have great knowledge of the magic arts and of healing. It is possible to become the blood-relative of a Vila when one helps her in trouble.

Those who want to become healers often use a very unusual ceremony to bring the Vily to them. A circle is drawn around the prospective healer with a birch-twig broom which was bought without bargaining. To be effective, the ceremony must take place before sunrise on a full-moon Sunday. In the middle of the circle two or three hairs from the mane, head and tail of a horse are placed, along with some manure, a horse's hoof and the flesh from under the hoof. The person inside the circle should then put his right foot on the hoof and yell loudly into his folded hands, 'Hu! Hu! Hu!' He should turn around the hoof three times, saying, 'Blood-sister Vily! I look for you over nine fields, nine meadows, nine lakes, nine woods, nine mountains, nine rocky mountain peaks and nine decaying castles, because you want to come to me and become my blood-sisters.'*

When the Vily come, they must be greeted, 'Blood-sisters! Vily! I've found you and am your beloved sister.' The 'sister' should then ask the Vily to grant his desires and tell them, 'What has belonged to me from the beginning of the world must be mine.'* They will be forced to grant the wish.

Identification: The majority of Vily have fair complexions, long reddish-brown curly hair that falls to their feet, and shimmering white clothes or coverings of green leaves. They sometimes have invisible wings which allow them to fly through the air. The Vily of the Yugoslavian–Hungarian border have slightly darker complexions, and die if they lose a single hair. The Yugoslavian coast Vily have iron teeth, goat's feet, and wear gold caps. The Bohemian Vily are called Jezinky. In Istria they are called Vili Čestitice, in Bulgaria Samovily. Only humans who are bound to the Vily as blood-relatives can call them by their proper names.

Like most wood spirits, Vily are not always of the same height. The Vily who live in the deep forest are larger and more formidable than those who live in the meadows that surround the forest. The Vily can most easily be recognized when they take the form of exquisitely beautiful girls in white dresses, or as Vila-horses. They have been seen as falcons and as silver wolves. Those born on Tuesday or Sunday can see Vily with most ease.

Habitat: Any tree can harbour a Vila. The Vila's life is bound to that of her host tree, though she may wander far away and not visit it for years. If a Vila-tree is cut down, a Vila will die, and her companions will come to avenge her death. The favourite trees of the Vily are fruit and nut trees, firs and beeches. They also live next to streams or in fabulous white fortresses and watch-towers on mountain-tops. Some live inside flax plants, but these flax Vily are very rare.

Vily live in eastern Europe.

A young boy was working in the fields. He had mowed all day but the work was dreary and boring. He stopped to look around and caught the eye of a girl working beside him. The Vila nodded at his silent question, and in a few moments, both had vanished from the field.

The boy's mother had just come from home with his dinner. When she failed to find him, she automatically suspected the worst and cried, 'The Vily must have taken my son! My poor boy, they've taken him away to the mountains, and I'll never see him again. Oh, my poor boy! Why did those wicked Vily have to take him away?'

She sobbed and howled over the fate of her son. Suddenly, she heard a Vila-voice beside her.

'You'd better thank God, woman, that my baby is sleeping on my lap. Otherwise I'd shoot you through with an arrow. You're an old bag, and don't understand anything about your son or about us. Now clear off before your yammering wakes the child!'

The woman didn't wait to hear more, but waddled home as quickly as she could.

Miodrag, peering through the trees of the thicket, saw a Vila milking her deer. He could barely keep from laughing when a buck mounted the doe the Vila was milking. The Vila, however, wasn't amused.

'You undisciplined beast! I hope Miodrag won't miss when he shoots at you!'

Miodrag didn't wait to be told twice. He had hunted the whole day without hitting a single animal and knew it was the Vila's fault. 'Then I won't miss!' he said, springing up from his hiding-place and felling the buck with a single shot.

'You're an even bigger beast than he was,' screamed the Vila. 'I hope your eye falls out as fast as you shot my buck!'

Before the words were out of her mouth, Miodrag had lost his right eye.

Two hunters were so proud of their knowledge of the mountains that they bet their companions that they would be able to count all the peaks of the Velež range. They set out early in the morning, climbed up to the top of one of the mountains and began to count. But try as they would, they couldn't do it. Each time, the score was different.

The day passed quickly and before they knew it, night had fallen. The hunters knew that Vily lived in the mountains, and might harm them if they were found sleeping there. They devised a method to fool the mountain women. They lay down very close to each other, head to foot, and wrapped the blanket around themselves in such a way that only their heads showed.

The Vily were, indeed, surprised when they found the strange sleepers in their forest.

'What kind of monster is this, sisters? By all the three hundred and seventy Velež mountain peaks, I've never seen a body with two heads!'

The men escaped from the Vily unharmed, and also won their bet.

While walking one day in the forest, Johannes fell through a hole in a bank, and broke his hand and his foot. A Vila materialized before him and offered to cure him, but for a price. She demanded that he pay one thousand ducats, and that his sister give up her kerchief, his brother his horse and falcon, his mother her silk supply, his father his arm, and his wife her pearl necklace. Johannes' father, mother, sister and brother agreed to pay the price, but his wife refused to give up her favourite necklace.

'If she can't pay, she certainly can't keep you!' grumbled the Vila.

Johannes' hand and foot refused to heal and his body was ravaged by fever. On the third day he died, a victim of his wife's greed.

'**M**ark my words, girl, you'll come to harm if you mess about with the Vily's well. They dug it, and won't let anyone near it.'

The girl, enchanted with the magic of the spring day, paid no attention to the old man.

'What magnificent flowers!' she exclaimed, picking the most beautiful of the Vily's roses. 'And this is just what I need,' she said, plunging her hand into the cool water.

As soon as she put the water to her lips, the Vily came. They were clothed in blinding white and walked menacingly toward the girl.

'You were warned not to drink from our spring, but were too feeble-minded to listen to good advice. Now pay for your stupidity!' cried the first, kicking her squarely in the throat.

'This is our spring, and no one can drink here,' said the second, tying the girl's hands behind her back.

'Don't ever come here again, or we'll kill you,' said the third, ripping out her eyes.

PORCUNES

THE *Portunes* were the very first English elves to be mentioned in writing and are among the few extinct species of elves. Nothing has been heard or seen of them for several centuries. The general tendency is to say that they have died out and will not appear again but it is possible that they have simply withdrawn from what they consider an evil and unjust world.

The Portunes were mainly remarkable for their size: they were about one inch high, even shorter than the Thumblings of children's 'fairy' tales. They came at night in great troops to invade deserted farmhouses, made themselves comfortable beside the fire and roasted tiny frogs in the flames for their supper. They were given to mischief, and often led travellers astray, laughing as the horses bogged down in the thick spring mud. But despite their high spirits, the tiny elves were welcomed wherever they went, for they were good workers and their presence invariably brought luck.

Identification: The Portunes were some of the smallest elves, ranging from half an inch to two inches in height. They were predominantly male, their faces were furrowed and wrinkled like those of old men, and their tiny coats covered with dozens of brightly coloured patches.

Habitat: The Portunes originally emigrated from France to England. They lived in farmhouses.

Leprechauns

THE Irish *Leprechaun* is the Faeries' shoemaker and is known under various names in different parts of Ireland: Cluricaune in Cork, Lurican in Kerry, Lurikeen in Kildare and Lurigadaun in Tipperary. Although he works for the Faeries, the Leprechaun is not of the same species. He is small, has dark skin and wears strange clothes. His nature has something of the manic-depressive about it: first he is quite happy, whistling merrily as he nails a sole on to a shoe; a few minutes later, he is sullen and morose, drunk on his home-made heather ale. The Leprechaun's two great loves are tobacco and whiskey, and he is a first-rate con-man, impossible to out-fox. No one, no matter how clever, has ever managed to cheat him out of his hidden pot of gold or his magic shilling. At the last minute he always thinks of some way to divert his captor's attention and vanishes in the twinkling of an eye.

Identification: Leprechauns and Cluricauns are small, between six and twenty-four inches high. They have light grey skin, old wrinkled faces and bright red noses. They wear three-cornered hats, old-fashioned green jerkins and waistcoats with enormous shiny buttons, leather aprons, long blue stockings and high-heeled shoes with silver buckles almost as big as the shoes themselves. They smoke small pipes and carry a leather purse. They are usually seen busily hammering a shoe.

Habitat: They live and work in quiet, secluded places. They make their homes under the roots of trees or in ruined castles. They live only in Ireland.

Although few people nowadays admit to a belief in the Faeries, at one time it was considered very dangerous for an Irishman *not* to believe in them. Felix O'Driscoll had drunk a little too much one night and said right out loud that he thought there were no Cluricauns, and that the stories about them were a lot of nonsense. An old woman was shocked by this talk.

'So you don't believe in what your ancestors never thought to doubt! Well, I'll tell you a thing or two. Cluricauns not only exist, but I've touched one!

'I was a young girl then, about to have my first child, and

A Leprechaun

I can tell you that was a good long time ago! I was pottering around a little in the garden when what should I hear but a sort of a hammering noise going knock, knock somewhere off among the beans. I couldn't imagine what it was, but it sounded a little like the sound the shoemaker makes when he's putting on a pair of heels. And sure enough, down there at the end of the beans was a little old man. He wasn't a quarter as big as a new-born child and had a cocked hat and a funny little pipe stuck in his mouth, puffing away at it so hard it would make a body laugh. His shoe buckles were so large that they covered his feet and he was working away as fast as he could. Well I knew then it was the Cluricaun, so I said to him, "It's an awful hot day for a person to be doing such hard work," and before I knew it, had him sitting in the palm of my hand. Then I pulled a horrible face and looked at him as wicked as I could and asked him where his sack of gold was. He sort of hemmed and hawed, and said he didn't know what a poor creature like himself would do with so much gold. So I got even meaner and pulled out the knife I had in my pocket, and told him I'd cut the nose right off his face if he didn't tell me. He got rather scared at that and said, "All right, come along and I'll show you where it is." I kept tight hold of him and my eyes right on him. We hadn't gone very far when I heard a lot of buzzing behind me. The Cluricaun yelled out, "Look, look, your bees are swarming!" and I was fool enough to look. I didn't see the bees and when I turned around, there wasn't anything in my hand, either. The little man had vanished just like smoke in the air, and I was tricked out of the gold.'

A long time ago, a farmer caught a Leipreachán hiding under a mushroom.

'Now I've got you! You won't get away until you've given me your gold!' The farmer threatened and cursed, but it did no good. The Leipreachán said he had no gold to give. The farmer then locked him up in a big dark trunk. Time passed and the Leipreachán didn't make a sound. One day, the farmer sold a piece of wood he had found washed up on the shore. That night the Leipreachán let out a loud laugh.

The Leipreachán stayed inside the trunk for seven years, and when he still wouldn't tell about the gold, was locked up for another seven.

Some time later a poor man came to the house but left without eating. The Leipreachán laughed again.

The next seven years soon passed and the Leipreachán refused once more to tell the farmer about the gold and was put back into the trunk. A little later, the farmer wanted to go to the fair, and dug up some money to take with him. When he came home that night, he heard the Leipreachán laugh loudly from the trunk.

'That's enough now,' said the farmer. 'You've laughed three times and I want to know what's so funny.'

After many arguments, the Leipreachán explained that he had laughed the first time because the wood the farmer had sold was full of gold. He had laughed the second time because the poor man had broken his leg on leaving the house. If he'd stayed and eaten, nothing would have happened. Then the Leipreachán told why he had laughed the last time. A thief had watched as the farmer dug up the money and had stolen the rest while the farmer was at the fair. The man went running out to the field to look for his money and when he found it gone, lost his mind as well.

As Thomas Fitzpatrick was out walking one fine autumn day, he heard a soft tapping noise coming from a hedge. Curious, he peered inside. In one corner he saw a brown jug, and next to it a little old man with a leather apron sitting on a stool and hammering on a tiny wooden shoe. Thomas had heard tell of Cluricans, but this was the first he had ever seen.

Very slowly, without taking his eyes from the shoemaker, he moved closer. When he was only a few inches away, he said, 'God bless the work, neighbour!'

The Clurican didn't seem at all surprised but answered him civilly and kept on with his work.

'And can I ask what you've got there in the jug?' Thomas asked.

'Beer, and good beer, made from heather tops,' said the Clurican.

Thomas laughed, but the Clurican seriously explained how the Danes had taught his great-grandparents the art of brewing heather beer.

'Could I try a little?' asked Thomas.

'Listen, young man, you should be at home herding the animals. Why, right now the cows have broken into the orchard and are trampling all your father's fruit.'

Thomas almost turned around but caught himself in time. 'You won't get away so easily,' he said and grabbed the little man. 'Tell me where your gold is.'

The Clurican led him over very rough country until they came to a field of ragwort plants.

'If you dig under this plant, you'll find all the gold you want.'

Thomas had of course brought no shovel with him, so he tied his red garter to the plant and ran home for a shovel.

'You won't be needing me any more, will you?' the Clurican asked.

'No, I suppose you can go now.'

When Thomas returned, every plant in the field had a bright-red garter tied to it and the Clurican had vanished.

SIRENS

Sirens are southern European sea spirits, similar to the northern European Mermaids, Havfrue and Meerweiber. They are gifted with such sweet melodious voices that they can enchant men, fish, and even the wind and water. Their power is at its strongest on moonlit nights, when they come to the surface to sing and dance in the silvery light, and at noon, when they hide themselves in the heat haze and lure ships on to reefs and rocks. Handsome young sailors should be especially careful: Sirens will do everything in their power to drown them and bring them to their underwater palaces. There the young men are jealously guarded and often tempted into marriage. Those who comply with the requests of the Sirens are treated kindly and live in greatest luxury, but those who refuse are kept prisoners and bound with golden chains.

The Sirens have the ability to change into fish, fish-women, bird-women and even birds. These talents were translated by the poets and myth-makers of Greek antiquity into the tale of the three Siren sisters who were punished by first being changed into bird-women, then into fish-women. They were fated to die if they let a single sailor pass them by unharmed, and killed themselves when tricked by Odysseus. Famous as it is, this story is merely a poetic and allegorical rendition of popular beliefs. The Sirens remain part of the fantastic fauna of many countries, despite this myth of their extinction. Various stories are still told of them and they have recently been sighted from the Azores to the Greek islands.

Identification: The Sirens are four to five feet tall. They are extraordinarily beautiful, wear rich gowns, and are very fond of jewellery. They sleep during the day and can only be seen at noon and in the light of the moon. When they travel through the water it is usually in the form of women with fish tails or as dolphins. When they travel through the air, they take eagle form.

The Greek Queen of the Sirens is a particularly dangerous and seductive spirit called the Lamia. In the Azores the Sirens are called Fate Marine.

Habitat: The Sirens live in sumptuous palaces under the sea, and are known on most of the Mediterranean islands, in Greece, Italy, France, Spain, Portugal and the Azores. They are rarely seen in the open sea, preferring to stay near river mouths or along coasts.

A headstrong boy had been warned by his mother not to go near the seashore because of the Lamia who lived there. He was too proud to take her advice and drove his sheep to the water's edge, sat down on a rock and began to play his pipes.

Instantly, the Lamia of the Sea appeared, and challenged him to a contest: his playing against her dancing. Whoever could dance or play longer would be the winner. The boy prided himself on his piping and his endurance, and foolishly accepted the challenge.

He played and she danced for three nights and three days. At the end of the third night the shepherd's strength gave way and he was forced to admit defeat. The Lamia of the Sea was still as fresh as she had been on the first day. She took his sheep and vanished into the sea, abandoning him there on the sand, more dead than alive.

MONACIELLI

THE Calabrian 'little friars' dress like monks but delight in pinching, teasing, throwing stones, knocking over wineglasses, breaking plates, scaring people, stealing bedcovers, cutting girls' braids, killing chickens, pounding on the walls, raising dust, ringing doorbells, dancing on sleepers' chests and making an unholy mess. They often take the form of cats and can move so quickly that it is very difficult to see them. They will only stay still if a sieve is placed next to them. Because they are very bad at arithmetic it takes them hours to count all the holes. While they are counting, no one will be bothered by their pranks.

The Sicilian Mamucca also dresses like a monk but has a sunnier disposition. His chief delight is hiding household items. The Sicilians say that 'Mamucca is having a whirl'* when something is missing, and do not trouble to look for it. As soon as everyone has calmed down, the Mamucca appears, smiling and holding the lost object.

Another Sicilian little friar is the Trapani Fratuzzo. He wears an enormous roof tile on his shoulders which hides him completely.

The best known of the little monks is the Neapolitan *Monaciello*. At one time many buildings in Naples stood empty because Monacielli were supposed to live there. These elves had such a bad reputation that no one dared to stay in the same house with them.

The little monks are all guardians of underground treasures and all wear red hoods. Anyone who has the luck to catch hold of one of their hoods has a chance to win the treasure. The monk whose hat has been stolen will do anything to regain it, since he cannot live without it. When he discovers it is gone, he will cry and howl, begging for its return. It should under NO circumstances be given back before the treasure is safely out of the ground. Once the monklet has his hat again, he will give a great shout of joy and run away without a second thought for promises or treasure.

Identification: The Calabrian Monachicchio is about ten inches tall and wears a red hood twice his own size. The Neapolitan Monaciello or Monachetto is one foot tall and wears a monk's habit and a red hood. His eyes are red and sparkle like fire. A similar Sardinian elf, the Pundacciú, has seven red hoods. If any one of these hoods is lost, the Pundacciú will die.

Habitat: These sprites are native to southern Italy but a few individuals have been seen as far away as Sardinia and Greece. They live inside houses but can occasionally be spotted in fields and caves.

A huge Neapolitan Orco and his wife were once sleeping peacefully when someone tried to steal their bedcovers. The Orco accused his wife of trying to keep them for herself and she accused him of taking them. But neither of them was to blame. When the Orco groped under the bed, he touched the face of the thief hiding there. Terrified that it might be his dreaded enemy the little monk, he cried out, 'The Monachetto! The Monachetto! The Monachetto is hiding under the bed! Help!'

In Calabria a story is told of a group of road workers. They started working early in the morning. By noon the sun was unbearable and they were ready for a break.

A Monaciello

After lunch, they lay down in a cave for a nap. None of them got any sleep, however, for the cave was inhabited by a Monachicchio who began to jump about, pinching and teasing them without mercy. The men tried every trick to capture him or his hood but he was too fast for them. Exhausted, they lay down again, appointing one man to stand guard. This was a fruitless tactic: the Monachicchio simply ran around the sentinel and pinched and teased as ruthlessly as before.

In their desperation, the men sent for the engineer. Surely an educated gentleman could think of a way of ridding them of the red-hooded pest! The engineer arrived, armed with two rifles. He fired one at the Monachicchio. The bullet hit the Monachicchio squarely in the chest but then ricocheted, almost killing the engineer. This was too much for the men, who fled in panic and never went to sleep in that cave again!

Poleviki and Poludnitsy

FIELD elves are fiercely jealous of their domains. They allow humans to harvest the crops, but only if the men know how to do it properly. The Noon Woman or *Poludnitsa* stops women she meets in the fields at noon, and interrogates them about the cultivation and spinning of flax. If the women don't know the answers, they have to pay with their lives. The Italian Pavaró slashes the legs of bean thieves, and the *Polevik* strangles drunkards foolish enough to trample through or fall asleep in his fields. Children who venture into the grain are led astray, or are suckled at the poisonous black breast of the Roggenmöhme or 'aunt-in-the-rye'. Her companion, the Pilwiz, sickens trespassers with elf-shot.

The over-protective nature of these elves has in recent years

A Polevik

been exaggerated and too much made of their jealousy. It should be remembered that each year our sickles and farm machinery cut down their fields, destroying their hiding-places, and sometimes even wounding them. When a farmer wanders into the fields at the wrong time and disturbs them, they react in kind, cutting his leg or his neck with an elfin sickle. It is therefore wise to know ways to discourage the vengeful elves. In Germany, one should throw a pocket knife with three crosses cut in it at the Pilwiz, yelling, 'There it is, Bilbze!' In eastern Russia, the bark of a certain tree will cure Polevik wounds, and some hold that anyone who can say the paternoster backwards for half an hour will not be bothered by elves.

Identification: The Russian field elves change their size in accordance with the field in which they live. In autumn they are only a few inches tall, in summer as high as the tallest plants in the field. The male Poleviki have dark skin, and dress in white linen. They have green hair. The females wear white, are very beautiful and appear at noon carrying sickles.

The German Pilwiz or Bockschitt, like the Polevik, has dark skin and dresses in linen. He comes out in the evening, a dark three-cornered hat on his head, a sickle tied to his left foot. His female companions, the Roggenmöhme, wear no clothes, showing their deadly black breasts. By far the most exotic-looking field elf is the Pavaró, a north Italian elf with fiery eyes, a wide mouth and a dog's head. He protects bean fields. His teeth are made of iron, as are his nails, and his arms are so long that they can sweep through several acres.

Habitat: The Poleviki are familiar throughout eastern and northern Europe and into Russia. The Swedish field elves are known as Lysgubbar. The Pilwize have spread from Bavaria to Poland and eastern Germany, Thuringia and Franconia. The Pilwize originally lived in trees, but have since moved into rye, oat and grain fields. The Pavaró lives only in broad-bean fields, the Korn-Kater in grain fields and the Bavarian Preinscheuhen in oat and millet fields.

ÐRΛKES

ALTHOUGH often confused with fire spirits, *Drakes* are house spirits who travel through the air as fiery streaks, bringing milk, grain and eggs to their masters. Their relationship with their masters is very intense, speaking of the violence of their natures. It is often a bond between two males, the male house Drake and his human master, and is occasionally signed in blood. To fulfil his part of the bargain, the Drake must take care of the horses and stables and make sure his master's pantry, granary, and gold chests are well stocked. The master must see to it that the Drake is well fed, and that all proper reverence is paid to him. Anyone who insults a Drake endangers the very existence of the house it lives in.

Drakes only take on the characteristics of fire when they fly. Then they appear as fiery stripes with great heads or as egg-shaped flaming balls. They can travel incredible distances in a fraction of a second and return just as fast, bringing gifts from halfway around the world. Humans who happen to see them on their journeys should get safely under cover, for they leave behind them an unbearable odour of burning sulphur. If the onlookers react quickly, they may succeed in gaining some of the gifts for themselves: they must quickly yell, 'Fifty-fifty!' or throw a knife at the Drake. If two people are present, they should cross their legs together in silence, pull the fourth wheel off a wagon and hurry under cover. If these rituals are performed quickly enough, the Drake will be compelled to drop part of his load.

Identification: The Drakes take on an almost overwhelming variety of shapes and forms. Although the northern European Drakes, Drachen, Draks and Fire-Drakes were originally, like some KOBOLDE, kept imprisoned inside carved mandrake roots, they now appear as small boys with red jackets and red caps and travel through the air as fiery streaks with large heads and long tails. The Swedish Krat appears as a small flying dragon, two to three feet high.

Habitat: The English, Scandinavian, German and French Drakes and Krats spend most of their time travelling through the air, but when at rest stay in the barn.

ASRAI

IN CHESHIRE and Shropshire, a full-moon night is called an *Asrai* night. It is then that the gentle, shy Asrai come to the surface of the water to look at the moon.

Though only the size of children, the Asrai are many hundreds of years old. They can only grow in the moonlight and can only surface once every century. If a single ray of sun touches them, they die immediately, melting into a pool of water. Their great enemy is man. Once a man has viewed their beauty, he tries to capture them.

Identification: Usually two to four feet high, they are always female and very beautiful, with long green hair and webbed feet. They wear no clothes and are benevolent and shy.

Habitat: They are English and live deep underwater, in cold lake-bottoms or in the sea. They cannot live on land.

A fisherman was out fishing one full-moon night when he felt something tugging at his nets. He pulled them in and saw the most beautiful girl he had ever set eyes on. She was an Asrai.

He couldn't bring himself to throw her back into the lake, so he dragged her up into the boat and covered her with rushes to keep her warm. She was as cold as ice and his hand burned where he had touched her.

He rowed to the other side of the lake, trying to ignore her crying. As he reached the opposite shore, the sun rose. The Asrai let out a scream. He turned to look at her but she was gone. The man had nothing to show for his night's work but a pool of water in the bottom of his boat and a paralysed hand.

Glashans and Shopiltees

As a rule the male lake spirits of northern Europe are monstrous and have nothing to do with the Little People. But there are exceptions to every rule.

The Scottish Kelpies and Fuaths take horse forms of gigantic size, but the Manx *Glashans* and the Shetland *Shopiltees* show themselves as miniature water horses. The Glashan appears as a small foal or a year-old lamb, while the Shopiltee is most often seen as a Shetland pony. Although less bloodthirsty than their larger relatives, they are always to be avoided. The Glashan is a woman-raper and the Shopiltee lives off the blood of those who drown.

Identification: The Glashan's true form is not known. He takes the shape of humans, lambs or grey foals. The Shopiltee is called Tangye in Orkney. Tangye is a small pony with horse's legs, enormous testicles and seaweed dripping from his back. He also appears as a human.

Habitat: They live in rivers and deep lakes in Wales, Scotland, Shetland and Orkney.

heinzelmännchen and hütchen

THE KOBOLDE were the original German home sprites, the NISSEN the first Scandinavian ones. Since those early days, they have been named and renamed, divided and subdivided into different subspecies. Two separate groups can now be picked out from the confusion of names. The first group is that of the POLTERSPRITES, noisy, bothersome spirits who owe their name to their perpetual racketing. The second includes those familiar elves who are so much a part of family life that they have been given nicknames. They are called Heinzlin or 'little Heinz', Hinzelmann or Heinzelmann, Guter Johann, Chimke (short for Joachim), and 'little Walter' or Wolterken; or are named Mützchen ('Capkin'), Eisenhütel, Hutzelmann, Pumphut, Hopfenhütel or *Hütchen* from the peculiar red cap that they wear.

This second tribe of sprites are extremely hard workers who will, for the limited payment of food once a week and on holidays, do almost all the house and farm work, wash the dishes, sweep and scrub the floors, curry, feed and water the horses, clean out the cow stalls, carry hay and corn into the barn, make fires, chop wood, discipline lazy servants, oversee the house and make sure misfortune does not touch their charges. Besides working they can also foretell the future and

A Shopiltee

give gifts of advice or magic. They are extremely loyal to their family and cannot be forced to leave the house voluntarily. There are several ways they can be pressed into leaving: if not fed, if continually insulted, if openly given gifts of clothes, if rushed at their work or laughed at, or if the house is burned down and a wagon wheel is left standing in front of it; but it must be borne in mind that they will leave angry, cursing those who have made them go.

Identification: The *Heinzelmännchen* and Hütchen are between one and three feet tall and wear green or red clothes with red hats. They often have red hair and beards and are occasionally blind. They have an infectious laugh, and are shape-changers, changing into cats, children, bats, snakes or roosters at will.

Habitat: All home sprites prefer to live in dark corners of the house, and the Heinzelmännchen and Hütchen are no exceptions. They can be found in the barn, the stable, the corner behind the oven, a tree near the house, in the roof beams, in the gables or in the cellar. They are inhabitants of Germany but have also been reported in Denmark.

One of the most famous German house sprites was Hinzelmann, a blond, red-hatted elf who lived with his wife Hille Bingels in Lüneburg in the middle of the sixteenth century. He had his room in the upper storey of the castle and furnished it with a pleated straw chair, a round table, a bed and a bedstead. Because of his usefulness around the house, he was allowed to eat at the dinner-table next to his master. Woe to the servant who forgot to bring him his dinner or his breakfast of crumbs and sweet milk!

Things had not always been so good at Lüneburg. At first, the master of the house was not at all happy with Hinzelmann. Many attempts were made to drive the sprite away but he

A Hütchen

would not go. If mistreated, he simply punished whoever had wronged him. When an exorcist was called, Hinzelmann tore up the prayer book and threw the pages around the room. Finally the lord of the castle called for his coach and left for Hanover. During the ride, a white feather floated along beside the carriage but the nobleman paid little attention. He was too busy congratulating himself on his escape from Hinzelmann.

Next morning, the noble discovered that he had not escaped at all. He woke up to find his golden neck-chain missing. Only after he had accused the innkeeper of stealing it and they had argued heatedly for several hours did Hinzelmann make his appearance. He told his master that he had followed him in the shape of a white feather from Lüneburg and had hidden the chain under the pillow. The nobleman then realized that he would never be able to rid himself of Hinzelmann, forgave him, and rode back with him to Lüneburg. For many years after that incident, Hinzelmann lived happily in the castle. When he left, it was with a promise to return in the final years of the noble's family.

Fate

THE Italian *Fate*, like the Irish Faeries, have a well-established and powerful aristocracy. Many of these high-born Fate are mentioned by name: the Fata Sibiana, the Fata Aquilina, the Fata Culina. Fata Alcina is the sister of the dreaded Fata Morgana, Queen of the French FÉES as well as of the Fate. She lives in splendour in a palace that shimmers in the air in the Straits of Messina. It is seen by sailors who then lose their lives in trying to reach it.

The Italian Fate are wood and water spirits of great beauty and kindness. They present their favourites with valuable gifts, but those who treat them rudely or cruelly pay for this thought-lessness with their beauty, health or good luck. Therefore it is always advisable to act modestly in the Fate's presence. It is not easy to recognize them for they are shape-changers and appear as old men or women, as beautiful young ladies or in the form of various animals. Those who stop to help an old woman in the forest often find to their great surprise that she isn't a woman after all but a Fata who rewards them liberally for their kindness.

Identification: The Fate are female elves, very beautiful and about five feet tall. They almost always dress in white. The Sibille of Abruzzo are treasure-guarding Fate and the Binidica of Sicily are benevolent and beautiful, although usually invisible.

Habitat: They live in caves, grottoes, rocks, springs or trees, which they protect from humans. They are most often seen at noon when their power is at its height. They live all over Italy as well as in Croatia.

Some girls from a small town near Torino were spinning one night. There was a full moon and the strange light started the girls talking of ghosts, Folletti and Fate.

One of them didn't want to listen to such talk.

'I want you to know I don't believe in Folletti, and as for your famous Fate – well, they're just old wives' tales! I'll go out there alone tonight and show you. They won't harm me 'cause they don't EXIST!'

Before the shocked girls could say anything, she had picked up her spindle and was out of the door. They called her and begged her to come back, but she didn't even turn round.

Her friends waited anxiously for her to return. The morning came but she did not. The girls organized a search party, and found what they expected. She lay under a giant chestnut tree, her spindle thrust through her heart.

Two half-sisters had been sent to fetch water. The daughter was given a jug but the stepdaughter was given a sieve. No matter how many times she dipped the sieve into the stream the water always ran out of it through the holes. Each time she brought the sieve home empty she was beaten by her stepmother.

One day it slipped from her hand and floated down the stream. The girl was terrified, because she knew she would be beaten mercilessly if she didn't bring it home. She started down the stream, asking all those she met if they had seen her sieve. Finally she found it, caught on an island of filth in the middle of the water. On top of the mound sat a filthy ugly old woman, picking lice from her hair.

'Please, if you can, would you give me my sieve?' asked the girl.

'Of course, dearie, but first you must see what is scratching my back,' the old woman answered. 'I just can't find out what it is.'

The girl killed the vermin that were swarming on the old woman's back, but told her that she had found diamonds and pearls.

'Then it's diamonds and pearls you'll have, young lady!' said the old woman, leading her into the house. 'Could you do another favour for me and make my bed?'

The girl agreed. Though the sheets were black with bedbugs, she told the old woman that the bed was full of roses and lilies.

'Then it's roses and lilies you'll have!' said the old woman.

The girl was asked to sweep the house. She did, and told the old woman that she had swept out rubies.

'Then it's rubies you'll have!'

The old hag led her over to a wardrobe and asked her to choose between a silk and a cotton dress.

'I'm just a poor girl, give me the cotton dress.'

'Then it's silk you'll get! Do you want a gold or a coral necklace?'

'Give me the coral.'

'Then it's gold you'll get! Do you want diamond or crystal earrings?'

'Give me the crystal ones.'

'Then it's diamond you'll have!' said the old woman, fastening two beautiful diamonds to her ears.

'From now on, you'll always be beautiful, and your hair gold. When you comb one side, roses and lilies will fall out, and when you comb the other side you'll have rubies. Now go home and don't turn round when you hear the donkey bray, but only when you hear the rooster crow.'

The girl turned around when the rooster crowed and a beautiful golden star appeared on her forehead.

Her half-sister was jealous of the girl's good luck and went to try for herself. She couldn't bring herself to be nice to the disguised Fata, and chose the wrong presents. When she came home, she was twice as ugly as before and had a donkey's tail in the middle of her forehead.

hey-hey men

FROM southern Germany and Czechoslovakia through parts of Poland, Hungary and Romania live a group of forest spirits called *Hey-Hey Men*. They are rarely seen but they are often heard, calling out, 'Hoy! Hoy! Hey! Hua!' Any traveller unfortunate enough to follow their echoing cry will certainly lose his way and any man foolish enough to mock the Hey-Hey Men will certainly lose his life.

The most famous Hey-Hey Man is the Rübezahl, a native of the Bohemian Riesengebirge. Like the Hey-Hey Men of Germany, he delights in leading people astray, but shows himself more often in a bewildering variety of shapes and forms. A woodcutter, a monk, a donkey, a charcoal burner, a guide, a messenger, farmer, hunter, horse or herb-gatherer met in the mountains can be the Rübezahl. Not only does he change his shape and make people lose their way, but he can also start rain-, hail- or snowstorms, make people's ears grow, change fruit into dung or into gold, give girls beards and men horns, change roots into snakes, lengthen people's noses, turn wigs into donkey-tails and make straw into horses. It is no wonder that he is called 'Master Johannes' and 'the Lord of the Mountains'.

Identification: The Rübezahl takes on so many disguises that it is impossible to distinguish his true form. The Hey-Hey Men can also change shapes but are most often visible as small men with large hats, their faces hidden, carrying whips and wearing red mantles. Among the many regional names for the Hey-Hey Men: the Bohemian Hejkadlo, the German Hoihoimann, Rôpenkerl and Hüamann, and the Romanian He-Männer and Schlorcherl, a swamp Hey-Hey Man.

Habitat: Originally the Hey-Hey Men only lived in deep forests, but since many of their favourite haunts have been cut down and destroyed they have moved into other desolate spots such as swamps, deserted millstreams and grain fields. The Rübezahl lives in the deeply wooded hills of the Bohemian mountains. The Hey-Hey Men can be found from the western parts of Germany into the Romanian mountains.

In England and France, the Hooters and Houpoux or Lupeux are mostly seen along the coast or in swamps and bogs.

A clever merchant once duped a simple farmer into buying a worthless piece of cloth for the price of fifty ducats.

Safe in the privacy of his store-room, the merchant's first impulse was to count his ill-gotten gold. He had been so eager for the money that he had not noticed that his victim was the Rübezahl and that the fifty ducats he had so greedily pocketed had been changed into a squirming mass of fur and teeth.

By that evening the merchant had caught the last mouse, but it was already too late. Of all his bolts of precious cloth, only one had been left intact. The others had tiny holes chewed in them by the 'gold mice' of the Rübezahl.

A thirsty man walked long until he found a pool of water. It was deep, so deep that it had a dark blue colour, so cold and clear that it could almost have been called black.

'So this is the famous pool of the Rübezahl!' the man exclaimed. 'Deep, dark, and dangerous. But if my friend Rübezahl doesn't mind, I'll help myself to a drink anyway.'

Hearing no answer, the man drank deeply and filled the water flask he always carried with him.

'Many thanks, friend!' he called out and started once again on his way.

After continuing his walk uphill in the summer sun, he began to feel the need for another drink. Unfastening his flask from his belt, he was surprised at how heavy it felt. When he tried to drink, not a single drop came out. In anger and frustration, he smashed the flask against a rock and found it filled with costly yellow topaz streaked with gold.

'Many thanks! I wish all my friends were as generous as you!' the man called out to the Rübezahl. Whether the Rübezahl heard him or not is not known, for he did not answer.

Angering the Rübezahl is something that should at all costs be avoided. A Bohemian woman once managed to insult him and had to pay dearly for her mistake.

She was very fond of make-up and happily bought a tin of purple shadow from a travelling salesman. It was only after she had put it on that she realized that the salesman had been the Rübezahl. The make-up was no ordinary cream. It was a poison which turned her skin a dark shade of brown. Try as she would, there was no way to remove the colouring and no make-up would mask it.

Salvanelli

IN CERTAIN northern Italian dialects, the word 'salbanello' or 'sanguanello' means the dancing reflection of sunlight in a mirror. It is also the name of a FOLLETTO. The *Salvanel* is a light-hearted and tricksy fellow, one of the smallest wood spirits. He herds large flocks of woolly sheep but never misses an opportunity to steal milk from other farmers. He tangles the manes and tails of horses and rides them so hard all night that they are not fit for work in the morning.

Another of his favourite pastimes is misleading travellers. He prances ahead of them up a mountain path and then vanishes with a laugh, leaving his victim at the edge of a precipice or high up on a narrow ledge. Those who inadvertently step on the Salvanel's footprints are also led astray. The only way to find the path again is to turn one's shoes around and walk with the toes pointing backwards.

Despite his playfulness, the Salvanel is not intentionally harmful. He loves to steal children (in particular, two- and three-year-old girls) but does it out of love for them and not

A Salvanel

out of hate or jealousy. They are raised with all possible care and tenderness in his cave deep in the woods.

Identification: The Salvanelli are three feet tall, sometimes smaller. They dress in red, have hairy reddish-brown skin, and are very lanky. They are the children of the SALVANI and the AGUANE. The children of the Salvanelli are called the Salbanelli.

Habitat: The Salvanelli live primarily in the Alps, but have been seen as far west as Genova and as far north as the Austrian Tirol. They live by preference in caves in the woods or inside trees.

After much planning, a Salvanel once stole a child from a neighbouring farm. It was only after he arrived home with the baby that he discovered that he had stolen a boy.

He was so upset that he ran all the way back to the farm. Bursting in on the unsuspecting parents, he yelled out, 'Take him back! Take him back! I don't want him! He's no girl!'

When the parents discovered what he was talking about, they were overjoyed to take the child away from the wildly gesticulating Salvanel.

A farmer had just finished milking his cows and the milk-can was left unguarded for a few minutes. When the man returned, the milk was gone.

Sure that the Salvanel had stolen his milk, the farmer decided to teach him a lesson. The next evening he filled the milk container with strong red wine and left it in the same place.

At first the Salvanel was puzzled by the exotic milk but then liked it so much that he drank himself senseless. When he came to, he was bound hand and foot.

'What plant gives such sweet juice, farmer?' the elf asked.

The suspicious man did not want to give him the right answer. 'Brambles,' he replied.

'I decree, then, that each bramble that touches the ground,' the Salvanel said, 'will grow new roots and make a new plant. Then there will be more juice for us all.'

The farmer swore under his breath at his own stupidity.

'I have one question for you, too,' said the farmer. 'Why do you steal my milk when you have the best herds in the country?'

'I drink your milk,' the elf replied, 'but with mine I make cheese.'

'Cheese?'

In return for his freedom, the Salvanel taught the man how to make cheese, butter and curds.

On his way out of the door, the Salvanel called out, 'Had you kept me a little longer, I would have taught you how to make wax out of the whey!'

To this day, many Alpine farmers still believe there is a way to make wax out of milk.

GWAGGED ANNWN

THE *Gwagged Annwn* or lake maidens are the most beautiful Welsh elves. Tall, proud, blonde and immortal, they live in rich palaces under Wales's many lakes, coming to land to dance, hunt or just stroll around, two or three at a time. On full-moon nights they rise from the ground a minute before midnight and dance lightly in the meadows until the first cock-crow in the morning. On many of these nights, only their heads can be seen, bobbing up and down over a soft field of silver mist.

The Gwagged Annwn are a very old race and for some reason not explained in legend are predominantly female. Because of this, they often look to handsome young men for companionship. The marriages between humans and Gwagged usually end unhappily for men, for the lake maidens only marry on difficult terms. For example, their husbands must never touch them with iron or hit them in any way, however lightly. Many young men marry them anyway, for their beauty is irresistible. Children of these unions are gifted with magic powers, and the elf women's dowries of fat lake cattle are rich prizes for penniless farmers.

Identification: The women are tall, fair, thin, with a light complexion. They range from four to six feet in height and can only be told from humans by their unearthly beauty and their inability to count beyond five. The males are old, with long white beards, handsome and strong even in old age. They are usually five feet tall. The German lake women are called Seefräulein and wear shimmering white dresses and veils. Their hair is blonde and their eyes blue, and they know the secrets of all the healing herbs.

Habitat: The Gwagged live in rich palaces under deep lakes. They are most often seen in Wales but similar elves have also been sighted in Brittany, England, Scandinavia, France and Germany.

The last sun-rays were reflecting off the surface of the lake with a warm golden glow as a young herdsman rounded up his mother's cattle.

He was on his way home when a form came floating towards him across the lake. It was a woman, beautiful beyond all his dreams, combing her long golden hair. The boy held his dinner of cheese and barley bread out to her and begged her to come and eat with him.

'Hard-baked is your bread! You won't find it so easy to catch me,' she whispered in a gentle voice and vanished quietly under the waves.

The next day the boy came again but brought uncooked dough with him. The light was fading when she finally approached, smiling softly.

'Your bread is unbaked! I won't have you!' she teased, vanishing with a light splash.

The next day she accepted his lightly baked bread, as well as his offer of marriage. Then she dived into the lake once again.

The young man was desperate – was she going to lead him on like this only to desert him? In his unhappiness, he decided to drown himself. Before he could, she reappeared, this time with an old man and another girl, just as beautiful as she was and identically clothed.

'To earn your bride, you must know which one she is,' the old man told him. 'If you choose correctly, she will be yours.'

After long study, the young man noticed that the girls were not identically dressed: one of the girl's sandals was tied differently. He was then able to recognize his bride.

Her father consented to the marriage on the condition that the young man not strike her 'three causeless blows'. Her dowry was set at the number of sheep, cattle, goats and horses she could count in one breath. In her soft voice she began to count, 'One, two, three, four, five; one, two, three, four . . .' until her breath gave way. The sum of these numbers then emerged as sheep from the lake and joined the young man's own flocks. The same ritual was observed for cattle, goats and horses. In the end, a large number of fat healthy animals stood on the shore.

The marriage was a happy one until one day the man hit his wife with a glove to hurry her on her way to a christening.

'The first blow has been struck! Take care!' she warned him.

He tapped her the second time at a wedding when she cried over the troubles the new couple would have to face. The third and final blow came much later, when their children were fully grown, at a funeral. The lake woman laughed loudly during the ceremony and her husband tried to stop her.

'You've struck me for the last time,' she cried. 'Now you won't see me again.'

She left, calling to all her animals. Even the black calf in the slaughterhouse came to life again and followed her into the lake.

But she did not neglect her sons. She taught the art of healing to the oldest one, Rhiwallon, and promised that his gift would stay in the family for many years to come. The skill of these doctors was famous, from Rhiwallon in the twelfth century through to the last Mydvai physicians of the nineteenth century.

GOAT PEOPLE

BESIDES various elves who occasionally take goat form or who have goat-like qualities, there is an entire group who have assumed the characteristics of both men and goats. The most famous of these are the Panes, Satyrs and Sileni of Classical Greece. These were early wood and field spirits who were later changed into the Classical half-gods with which we are familiar. The Sileni or Albanian *Goat People* were reduced to Silenus, the drunken old goat-man who followed Dionysos. The Satyrs, once known only in Argos, were suddenly recognized all over Greece as the 'gentle gods'. The wood and herd Panes were telescoped into 'the great god Pan', the pipe-playing nymph-ravager.

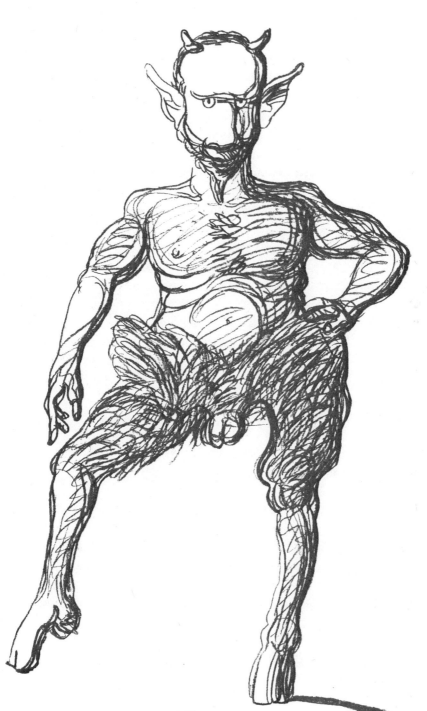

A Satyr

In Italy the Goat People were called Fauni and Silvani. The Fauni, once field spirits who gave nightmares to animals, were honoured at state festivals and were changed into the god Faunus. The Silvani, elves who guarded the herds, houses and land boundaries of the ancient Romans, became the minor god Silvanus.

These newly mythologized gods replaced the old Satyrs and Fauni in the minds of the people. The original Goat People were forgotten and not even recognized when they were seen. It is only lately that there has been talk of new elves, the descendants of the ancient Goat People. There have been reports of Panes seen by mountain shepherds in Greece, and the Italian SALVANI and SALVANELLI are very similar to the old Silvani.

Identification: The Goat People appear with goat feet and legs and a man's upper body. The Greek Goat People are superb dancers and are covered with rough goat fur. The Sileni look older than the Satyrs and Panes. The Satyrs have extraordinarily large genitals, flat noses and pointed ears.

The Italian Fauni and Silvani are physically very similar to the Greek elves. The Fauni are of small stature, the Silvani and SALVANI larger, with thick body fur. They are very strong.

Habitat: The Sileni were originally Albanian spirits, and the Satyrs came from Argos. Later they spread to other parts of Greece. The Fauni and Silvani lived in Italy, ranging to the Swiss and French Alps.

The Goat People prefer to live in light, airy woods and fields. They travel with the breezes and have some control over the movements of the wind.

MASSARIOU

THE Veneto *Massariol* is, true to his name, a 'little farmer', small, jolly and fat, with a large red hat. He cares for the horses and cattle. His favourite animals can easily be recognized by their size, for he fattens them enormously in the course of a single night. If the manes of the horses and the tails of the cows are found braided on Saturday, it is a sure sign that a Massariol is grooming them.

His activities are not limited to the barn. He also helps in kitchens, close to the women he fancies. He is a ladies' man, often changing himself into a comb or a thread in order to be closer to their bodies. He takes great delight in watching young girls and sometimes leads them high up into the mountains and forces them to dance for his benefit. When they are tired, he carefully brings them back home, unharmed but weary.

Identification: The Massariol is one foot high and dresses in red with red knee-socks and a large red hat. He has a horse's laugh and an old man's face.

The Yugoslavian 'land Maćić' or Mamalić is very closely related. The 'sea Maćić' is a Maćić who has a weakness for doughnuts and lives in the sea.

Habitat: The Massariol lives on the plains of north-eastern Italy on large collective farms. He lives in smaller households in the southern Alps. He is to be found as far south as Krk in Yugoslavia and as far north as the Italian Dolomites.

A Massariol was once discovered feeding the cows. In gratitude, the farm workers made him a shirt and left it in the barn one night. But when the Massariol saw it, he cried out, 'I have one foot here, and one foot there, and your shirt just *won't* do!'

A Yugoslavian Mamalić lived in the ceiling of a country house and loved *maccheroni*. He had made an agreement with the owners of the house that if they would give him a plate of pasta every day, he would pay them with gold coins.

A serving girl was once asked to carry his plate up to him but was so hungry that she gobbled down all the food before reaching the top of the stairs.

The Mamalić had been watching her. As she started to climb back down the stairs, he tangled himself up in her legs and sent her crashing to the bottom.

Her master came running at the sound and found her at the foot of the stairs, the empty plate next to her head. A new pot of *maccheroni* was quickly put on the fire before the angry Mamalić had time to do more damage.

A small sea Maćić came to the beach one day where a widow was walking. When she agreed to fry some doughnuts for him he vanished, returning quickly with a golden fish. Each time she fried doughnuts for him, he gave her more gold.

'And what is your name, you who cook so well?' asked the Maćić.

'Myself,' replied the clever woman.

She continued to work at the stove for the gold-bearing Maćić. One day she was so bored that she let the pan of hot oil fall on the sprite.

Howling with pain and anger, he raced down to his friends the land Maćićs.

'Who did this to you?' they demanded.

'Myself did it!' the sea Maćić howled. 'Myself burnt me!'
The poor Maćić barely escaped a beating for his stupidity.

ᴎᴇʀᴇɪᴅᴇꜱ

THE *Nereides* or Exoticas are most dangerous at noon and at
midnight. Any man who disturbs their noon meal or who
falls asleep near their favourite spots will regret his action.
He will be afflicted with insanity, sickness, impotence or death.
If he watches them bathing, they will blind him, and if he
talks to them, they will take his voice.

Many young men try to gain the Nereides as wives by
capturing their white shawls. Without her shawl, the Nereid's
life is meaningless and she will remain with the man. If she
can regain her shawl, she will run away to join her companions
and dance with them on the hilltops. The children left behind
retain many of their mothers' traits. Some Greek villagers can
still point out residents who are of Nereid descent.

There are several ways of avoiding the anger and bad will
of the Nereides. It is customary to treat all whirlwinds with
respect and to greet them with the charm, 'Milk and honey in
your path!'* since the Nereides often travel in them. It is
not safe to be found outside the house at noon or at midnight.

Women must take special precautions against the Nereides
after childbirth. In their jealousy, the elves will try to harm
or sicken the woman, or steal her child. The woman should
under no circumstances make noise at night, or they will
discover her hiding-place. When leaving the house she should
take care always to step on the door-key. A black cross should
be painted on the threshold and food laid out for the Nereides.

If a man or woman has been 'struck' by the Nereides or
harmed in any way by them, he should wait a week, a month
or a year and then go to the place where the accident occurred,

at exactly the same time of day. Offerings (particularly of honey) should be left for the Nereides. Those leaving the gifts should not look back after setting the food down, or the Nereides will be offended anew.

Identification: The Nereides or 'honeyed ones' are always beautiful. They are young, slender, graceful, have milk-white skin and a beautiful voice, and dress in white and gold. A white shawl is draped over their heads and shoulders or carried in their hands. They are not immortal, for 'a crow lives twice as long as a man, and a tortoise twice as long as a crow, and a Nereid twice as long as a tortoise'.* Occasionally they have one horse's or ass's foot. They can fly through the air and pass through knot-holes in wood. They are mostly female.

Habitat: At one time the Nereides were called Nymphs and were classified as Naiades, Oreades, Dryades, Limniades, etc., according to their various residences. As these many varieties of Nymphs changed homes and mated with spirits, men and gods, they could no longer be so easily categorized.

Today they are called Nereides or Exoticas, and those who live in the mountains cannot be told apart from those who live in rivers. They are known throughout Greece, Albania and Crete, and live in the sea, in rivers, springs, wells, mountains, caves, high peaks, valleys, plains, trees and small rocks. The Albanian Exoticas are called Jashtesmé.

A young man of Crete was invited by the Nereides to play the lyre in their cave. The face of the youngest haunted him for days afterwards. He decided to make her his wife at any cost and sought the advice of a wise woman. She told him that he must go to them again and stay in the cave until morning. Just before cock-crow, he must grab the girl by the

A Nereid

hair and hold her tightly. No matter what shapes she changed into, he must continue to hold her.

The young man was so infatuated with his Nereid that he followed the old woman's advice. He held on to the Nereid even though she changed into a dog, a snake, a camel and a live flame. At the crowing of the black cock, the other Nereides vanished. The elf had no choice but to stay with the young man.

They lived together for a few years, and she had a child. Her husband was troubled by the fact that she never spoke, and went to the old wise woman once again.

'To make her talk, you must take her child and pretend to throw it into the oven. You can be sure she'll talk then!'

The man did as he was told. When the mother saw flames next to her child, she screamed, 'Let go of my child, you dog!' Then she vanished with the baby in her arms. He had made her speak for the first and the last time. He never saw her again.

A young girl set out late one night for the neighbouring flour mill. It was already midnight when she arrived and the miller was fast asleep. But the mill was not empty: the Nereides were having a party there. As soon as they saw the girl, they seized her and dressed her in a white bridal gown and a golden crown – what better time for a wedding party! They then left the girl in the care of an old elf while they rushed away for the bridegroom.

The girl had no intention of becoming a Nereid's bride, and managed to give the old man the slip, escaping with her donkey and two sacks of grain.

When the Nereides returned and couldn't find her, they were angry. They rushed down the path to the village to see if they could discover any traces of her. Soon they came to the donkey but couldn't find the girl.

'That is one sack and that is the other, and that is the middle sack. Where is the girl?' they asked.

They stormed back to the mill to make sure she hadn't hidden there. The girl then jumped down from where she had concealed herself on the donkey's back and hurried down the path. She soon had to hide again, for the Nereides returned after they had found nothing at the mill.

'That is one sack and that is the other, and that is the middle sack. Where is the girl?'

They didn't find her this time either. This ritual continued all night until the frustrated Nereides were forced to leave when the white, the red and the black cocks crowed. The girl was safe, and had the costly golden crown.

Her sister was so envious of her luck that she decided to try for herself. But the Nereides were not about to be fooled *this* time. They didn't let the jealous sister out of their sight and she was never seen in the village again.

Fées

The Buschgrossmutter

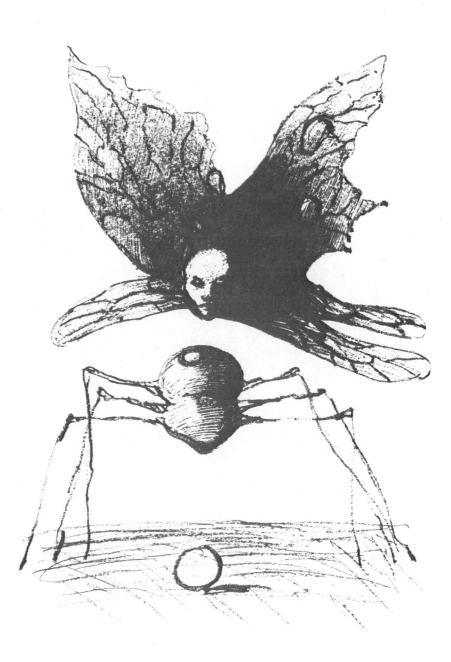

Lutins

A Linchetto

The Barabao

A Church Grim

Tree Elves

A Skovmann

A Fylgia

A Fountain Woman

A Dame Vert

Night-Elves

One of the Alven

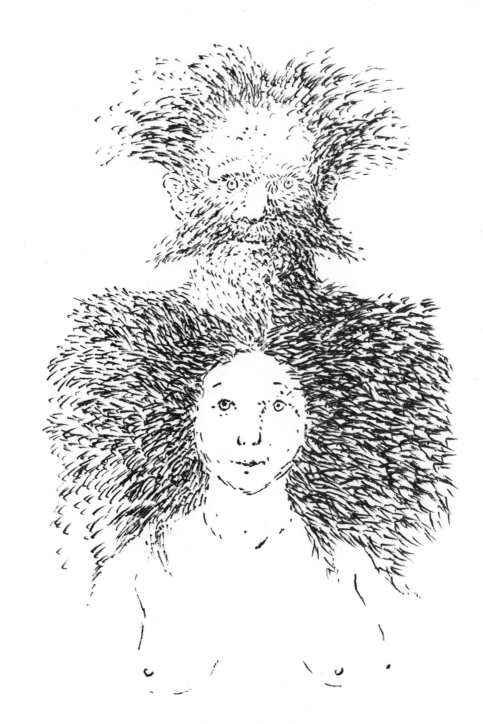

A Salvan and an Aguana

A Fata

A Seliges Fräulein

One of the Sleigh Beggey

A Laúru

A Kornbock

A Portune

NOTES

11   *each other'*. W. W. Gill, *A Manx Scrapbook* (London, 1929), vol. 1, p. 16.

20   *for ever'*. Lady Gregory, *Visions and Beliefs in the West of Ireland*, 2 vols (London, 1920), vol. 2, p. 200.

20   *the better for it'*. Ibid., vol. 2, p. 189.

22   *A woman ... worn away.* From W. B. Yeats, *Mythologies* (London, 1959), p. 76.

22   *As she was ... her daughter away.* From Gregory, *Visions and Beliefs*, vol. 1, p. 193.

23   *A young boy ... at every turn.* From ibid., vol. 1, p. 14.

23   *A small shepherd's cottage ... bothered her again.* From ibid., vol. 2, p. 21.

25   *Clumsy Thorsten ... quite a sight.'* From Benjamin Thorpe, *Northern Mythology*, 3 vols (London, 1852), vol. 1, p. 114.

26–8   *The cows ... half-forgotten visions.* From Thomas Keightley, *The Fairy Mythology* (London, 1968), p. 90.

32   *A boy ... the same year.* From Johann Nepomuk Ritter von Alpenburg, *Mythen und Sagen Tirols* (Zürich, 1857), p. 97.

40   *'Be careful ... their escape.* From *Schweizerisches Archiv für Volkskunde* (Zürich, 1897–　), vol. 26, p. 71.

42   *In the last century ... twisted off.* From Ludwig Bechstein, *Deutsches Sagenbuch* (Leipzig, 1853), p. 470.

44   *It was the day ... a tiny dwarf.* From Ernst L. Rochholz, *Schweizersagen aus dem Aargau*, 2 vols (Aarau, 1956), vol. 2, p. 324.

44   *In a small town ... a costly jewel!* From Ernst L. Rochholz, *Naturmythen* (Leipzig, 1862), p. 126.

44–5   *A poor serving girl ... her life.* From Rochholz, *Schweizersagen*, vol. 2, p. 312.

45–6   *It was common knowledge ... the golden cheese.* From Bechstein, *Deutsches Sagenbuch*, p. 17.

46   *Poor people ... off a cliff.* From Rochholz, *Naturmythen*, p. 107.

50–2   *A ferryman ... until his death.* From Bechstein, *Deutsches Sagenbuch*, p. 621.

52   *A Wichtl ... his lost love.* From von Alpenburg, *Mythen*, p. 107.

55–6   *'Please take me ... a hundred miles away.* From Bechstein, *Deutsches Sagenbuch*, p. 526.

56-8 *It was a hot day . . . in health and peace.* From Friedrich Ranke, *Die deutschen Volkssagen* (Munich, 1910), p. 130.

58-9 *A poor woman . . . gold coins.* From Bechstein, *Deutsches Sagenbuch,* p. 758.

59-60 *It was 1883 . . . nightly visitors.* From *The Folk-Lore Journal* (London, 1888-   ), vol. 1, p. 361.

60 *A farmer . . . with their jealousy.* From Thorpe, *Northern Mythology,* vol. 3, p. 37.

62-4 *While spinning . . . in the cellar.* From Bechstein, *Deutsches Sagenbuch,* p. 451.

64-5 *A Danish family . . . by a changeling again.* From Keightley, *The Fairy Mythology,* p. 125.

68-9 *A hunchbacked farmer . . . with holy water.* From Patrick Kennedy, *Legendary Fictions of the Irish Celts* (London, 1866), p. 104.

69-70 *A Cornish woman . . . to be seen again.* From *The Folk-Lore Journal,* vol. 5, p. 184.

75 *Two fishermen . . . in any way!* From Paul Sébillot, *Le Folk-Lore de France,* 4 vols (Paris, 1904-7), vol. 2, p. 113.

75-6 *A Corsican . . . seven generations.* From ibid., vol. 2, p. 414.

76 *The inhabitants . . . war or plague.* From Wilhelm Mannhardt, *Antike Wald- und Feldkulte* (Berlin, 1877), p. 175.

78 *a red egg!'* W. R. S. Ralston, *The Songs of the Russian People* (London, 1872), p. 135.

78 *the new spot!'* Ibid., p. 138.

80 *On a lonely hill . . . the old stove.* From ibid., p. 123.

80 *A southern Polish house . . . go hungry.'* From ibid., p. 124.

81 *One day . . . the cat again.* From ibid., p. 132.

82-3 *'This is the last money . . . a good bargain.* From ibid., p. 131.

84-6 *Richard . . . bragged again.* From Kennedy, *Legendary Fictions,* p. 91.

86 *A woman was walking . . . that evening!* From Gregory, *Visions and Beliefs,* vol. 1, p. 14.

86-7 *The Faeries . . . the day she died.* From Sean O'Sullivan, *Folktales of Ireland* (London, 1966), p. 176.

87-8 *Ragweed stalks . . . her neighbour again.* From Gregory, *Visions and Beliefs,* vol. 1, p. 85.

90 *The Tylwyth Teg . . . in the house again.* From John Rhys, *Celtic Folk-lore,* 2 vols (Oxford, 1901), vol. 1, p. 37.

90-1 *In the eighteenth century . . . the rest of her life.* From ibid., vol. 1, p. 211.

91-2 *The Tylwyth Teg . . . from home.* From ibid., vol. 1, p. 104.

93-4 *The plague . . . left Switzerland.* From Wilhelm Mannhardt, *Der Baumkultus der Germanen und ihrer Nachbarstämme* (Berlin, 1875), p. 97.

94   *The Nörglein ... haunting cry.* From Johann Nepomuk Ritter von Alpenburg, *Deutsche Alpensagen* (Vienna, 1861), p. 48.

94–5 *In the middle ... the first thaw.* From von Alpenburg, *Mythen*, p. 91.

96–7 *A rich and powerful count ... never seen again.* From Ignaz and Josef Zingerle, *Tirols Volksdichtungen und Volksgebräuche* (Innsbruck, 1852), vol. 1, p. 226.

99–100 *The Saal River Nixie ... I will kill you.'* From Bechstein, *Deutsches Sagenbuch*, p. 463.

100–1 *As was their custom ... see us again!'* From Sébillot, *Le Folk-Lore*, vol. 2, p. 349.

102   *in the water.'* Thorpe, *Northern Mythology*, vol. 2, p. 112.

103   *The wise woman ... man or woman.'* From Johannes Wilhelm Wolf, *Deutsche Märchen und Sagen* (Leipzig, 1845), p. 195.

103   *A Westphalian man ... with a cry underwater.* From Keightley, *The Fairy Mythology*, p. 260.

104   *Some Swedish farmers ... with the Neck.* From Thorpe, *Northern Mythology*, vol. 2, p. 79.

104   *Several young men ... into the water.* From ibid., vol. 3, p. 28.

106–8 *A fifth-century woman ... with fewer scruples.* From Ludovico Maria Sinistrari, *Demoniality* (London, 1927), p. 15.

108–9 *In many Alpine villages ... broken-hearted.* From Maria Savi-Lopez, *Alpensagen* (Stuttgart, 1893), p. 209.

111–2 *A Dane ... his master's house.* From Keightley, *The Fairy Mythology*, p. 118.

112–3 *Although the Huldre Folk ... a piece of wire.* From Thorpe, *Northern Mythology*, vol. 2, p. 16.

113–4 *It was late summer ... end of the valley.* From ibid., vol. 2, p. 6.

116   *A Mermaid ... many years to come.* From John Brand, *Observations on the Popular Antiquities of Great Britain*, 3 vols (Detroit, 1969), vol. 3, p. 413.

116–7 *It is common knowledge ... rabid alley-cats.* From R. Macdonald Robertson, *Selected Highland Folk-Tales* (London, 1961), p. 159.

117–8 *A group of Irish immigrants ... the New World.* From Gregory, *Visions and Beliefs*, vol. 1, p. 11.

119–20 *Grethe often came ... left behind.* From Thorpe, *Northern Mythology*, vol. 2, p. 172.

122   *A Herefordshire Hobgoblin ... over the fire.* From K. M. Briggs, *The Fairies in Tradition and Literature* (London, 1967), p. 35.

124–5 *Several men ... into the woods.* From ibid., vol. 3, p. 203.

125   *A Russian man ... white horse.* From Ralston, *Songs*, p. 134.

128   *The kingdom ... cartload of gold.* From Bertha Ilg, *Maltesische Märchen und Schwänke*, 2 vols (Leipzig, 1906), vol. 1, p. 100.

130   *Two girls ... cut off.* From Keightley, *The Fairy Mythology*, p. 477.

130–1 *It was customary . . . the milk had vanished.* From *Schweizerisches Archiv,* vol. 18, p. 113.

131 *Nobody could believe . . . rid of the beast.'* From ibid., vol. 18, p. 112.

131–2 *Two fishermen . . . all my fun!'* From Sébillot, *Le Folk-Lore,* vol. 2, p. 89.

134 *The Pixies . . . the rest of its life.* From Ruth L. Tongue, *Somerset Folklore* (London, 1965), p. 112.

134–5 *An Exmoor farmer . . . had done before.* From ibid., p. 117.

138–9 *A man once passed . . . had vanished.* From Bechstein, *Deutsches Sagenbuch,* p. 609.

139 *A Kobold . . . on the cart.* From Thorpe, *Northern Mythology,* vol. 3, p. 84.

142 *The year 1843 . . . hundreds of miles away.* From Ralston, *Songs,* p. 156.

142–3 *A woman . . . pure gold!* From Mannhardt, *Baumkultus,* p. 142.

143 *'Good day . . . Ha! Ha! Ha!'* From Ralston, *Songs,* p. 158.

144 *The Leshiye . . . the obliging Leshy.* From Mannhardt, *Baumkultus,* p. 140.

145–6 *Two fiddlers . . . one hundred years long.* From Keightley, *The Fairy Mythology,* p. 380, and Robertson, *Selected Highland Folk-Tales,* p. 9.

146–7 *The Beansìth . . . never visited her again.* From ibid., p. 12.

147 *After a long walk . . . the Beansìth.* From J. F. Campbell, *Popular Tales of the West Highlands,* 4 vols (Edinburgh, 1860-2), vol. 2, p. 68.

148 *An old Scottish ballad . . . elfin wood!'* From R. Brimley Johnson (ed.), *A Book of British Ballads* (London, 1966), p. 83.

149 *pay you back!'* 'Carobole, carobole, doman te pagheró.' Giuseppe Bonomo, *Studi Demologici* (Palermo, 1970), p. 129.

149–50 *A poor Venetian . . . into her house!'* Giuseppe Bernoni, *Leggende fantastiche popolari veneziane* (Venice, 1875), p. 22.

153–4 *The Kaboutermannikins . . . without success.* From Wolf, *Deutsche Märchen,* p. 342.

154–6 *It is a well-known fact . . . rich man today!'* From Bechstein, *Deutsches Sagenbuch,* p. 140.

158 *A man was returning . . . the Aguana was saved.* From Christian Schneller, *Märchen und Sagen aus Wälschtirol* (Innsbruck, 1867), p. 211.

158–9 *Tired from his day's work . . . the Bregostano's expense.* From ibid., p. 226.

160–1 *A little girl . . . by the Farises.* From K. M. Briggs and Ruth L. Tongue, *Folktales of England* (London, 1965), p. 34

161 *Cakes . . . high-heeled shoes.* From Keightley, *The Fairy Mythology,* p. 305.

161–2 *An Oxfordshire man . . . a poor and bitter man.* From Tongue, *Somerset Folklore,* p. 154.

164   *A miller . . . became his helper.* From Savi-Lopez, *Alpensagen*, p. 204.

165   *makes the horse fat'.* Thorpe, *Northern Mythology*, vol. 2, p. 94.

168   *A boy . . . into the gutter.* From Keightley, *The Fairy Mythology*, p. 146.

168–9 *Because of similarities . . . jaws of the hounds.* From ibid., p. 142.

172–3 *A group of Shetland seal hunters . . . as she swam.* From Samuel Hibbert, *A Description of the Shetland Isles* (Edinburgh, 1822), p. 160.

174   *A Laüru . . . only broken shards.* From Giuseppe Gigli, *Superstizioni, pregiudizi e tradizioni* (Bologna, 1970), p. 49.

176   *A drunken servant . . . the house snake.* From Bernhard Schmidt *Das Volksleben der Neugriechen und das Hellenische Alterthum* (Leipzig, 1871), p. 187.

176–8 *A poor farmer . . . saw Rarash again.* From John Naake, *Slavonic Fairy Tales* (London, 1874), p. 257.

180   *A poor man . . . her other presents.* From Mannhardt, *Baumkultus*, p. 85.

180   *Yew travels late'.* Tongue, *Somerset Folklore*, p. 26.

181   *in the forest'.* Mannhardt, *Baumkultus*, p. 10.

181   *forget my child!'* Ibid., p. 65.

182   *A successful Derbyshire farmer . . . a long life.* From Ruth L. Tongue, *Forgotten Folk-Tales of the English Counties* (London, 1970), p. 150.

183   *In Balla Koig . . . their night-fought battle.* From Gill, *A Manx Scrapbook*, vol. 1, p. 207.

186   *A fisherman . . . out of the boat.* From Ralston, *Songs*, p. 151.

186   *A north Russian Vodyany . . . never to be seen again.* From *New Larousse Encyclopedia of Mythology* (London, 1968), p. 292.

187   *on his face!'* Bonomo, *Studi Demologici*, p. 123.

188   *A Lucchese boy . . . from the house.* From *Bollettino storico lucchese* (Lucca, 1935), p. 38.

189   *A brown-haired girl . . . stalked out.* From Bonomo, *Studi Demologici*, p. 123.

192   *A Rusalka . . . upon the shore.* From Ralston, *Songs*, p. 150.

193   *please a Brownie'.* William Henderson, *Notes on the Folk-lore of the Northern Counties of England and of the Borders* (London, 1879), p. 248.

194–6 *Most Brownie stories . . . no man could.* From ibid., p. 266.

196   *A Berwickshire Brownie . . . again in Scotland.* From ibid., p. 249.

196   *Another mischievous Brownie . . . has't a'!'* From Keightley, *The Fairy Mythology*, p. 359.

197–8 *A Bwca . . . to the Red Sea.* From Rhys, *Celtic Folklore*, vol. 2, p. 594.

202   *Twilight was fading . . . subsided.* From Mannhardt, *Baumkultus*, p. 113.

202–3 *'When I was young . . . trusted a man.'* From ibid., p. 135.

209   *A girl had a year ... happily obeyed.* From Bernhard Schmidt, *Griechische Märchen, Sagen und Volkslieder* (Leipzig, 1877), p. 66.

209–10 *The midwife ... the Rojenice.* From Anton von Mailly, *Sagen aus Friaul und den Julischen Alpen* (Leipzig, 1922), p. 19.

212   *driven away the Seligen.*' 'Die Welt is halt anders geworden, aber nit besser. Die Wilden Männer sind in das Land gekommen, und haben die Seligen vertrieben, und a-hi-gethan, davon weiss man viel zu derzäll'n.' Von Alpenburg, *Mythen*, p. 8.

214   *During haying ... his dying day.* From Mannhardt, *Baumkultus,* p. 105.

214–5 *A bold young man ... blinding him.* From von Alpenburg, *Mythen,* p. 18.

216   *The Wild Hunt ... in his mind.* From ibid., p. 29.

216–7 *A Selige ... not seen again.* From ibid., p. 23.

218–20 *A Mallorcan miller's wife ... expect their grain.* From Erzherzog Ludwig Salvator, *Märchen aus Mallorca* (Leipzig, 1896), p. 151.

222   *Lord Nann ... was also dead.* From Keightley, *The Fairy Mythology,* p. 433.

224–5 *A Swiss Poltersprite ... without interruption.* From *Schweizerisches Archiv,* vol. 12, p. 48.

225   *a bad Vila.*' 'Ob die Vila weiss, ob schwarz ist, eine Vila bleibt immer eine böse Vila.' Friederich Krauss, *Volksglaube und religiöser Brauch der Südslaven* (Münster, 1890), p. 90.

226   *my blood-sisters.*' Ibid., pp. 104–6.

227   *must be mine.*' Ibid., p. 79.

228   *A young boy ... as she could.* From ibid., p. 99.

228–9 *Miodrag ... his right eye.* From ibid., p. 85.

229   *Two hunters ... won their bet.* From ibid., p. 79.

229–30 *While walking ... his wife's greed.* From ibid., p. 95.

230   '*Mark my words ... ripping out her eyes.* From ibid., p. 87.

232–4 *Although few people ... out of the gold.*' From Crofton Croker, *Irische Elfenmärchen* (Frankfurt, 1966), p. 82.

234–5 *A long time ago ... his mind as well.* From O'Sullivan, *Folktales of Ireland,* p. 179.

235–6 *As Thomas Fitzpatrick ... the Clurican had vanished.* From Croker, *Elfenmärchen,* p. 91.

238   *A headstrong boy ... more dead than alive.* From Schmidt, *Volksleben,* p. 132.

239   *having a whirl*'. Giuseppe Pitré and S. Salomone-Marino, *Archivio per lo studio delle tradizioni popolari,* 23 vols (Palermo, 1882–9), vol. 20, p. 536.

240   *A huge Neapolitan Orco ... Help!*' From Gian Alesio Abbatius, *Il Pentamerone del Cavalier Giovan Battista Basile* (Naples, 1728), p. 126.

240–2 *In Calabria . . . in that cave again!* From Carlo Levi, *Cristo si é fermato a Eboli* (Turin, 1958), p. 135.

247 *A fisherman . . . a paralysed hand.* From Tongue, *Somerset Folklore,* p. 25.

250–2 *One of the most famous . . . the noble's family.* From Keightley, *The Fairy Mythology,* p. 240.

253–4 *Some girls . . . through her heart.* From *Guida all'Italia leggendaria misteriosa insolita fantastica,* 2 vols (Milan, 1967), vol. 1, p. 430.

254–5 *Two half-sisters . . . in the middle of her forehead.* From Italo Calvino, *Fiabe italiane,* 2 vols (Turin, 1956), vol. 1, p. 409.

257 *A clever merchant . . . the Rübezahl.* From Bechstein, *Deutsches Sagenbuch,* p. 534.

257 *A thirsty man . . . did not answer.* From ibid., p. 533.

258 *Angering the Rübezahl . . . would mask it.* From ibid., p. 535.

260 *After much planning . . . the wildly gesticulating Salvanel.* From Schneller, *Märchen,* p. 214.

260–1 *A farmer had just finished . . . out of milk.* From ibid., p. 213.

262–4 *The last sun-rays . . . the nineteenth century.* From Rhys, *Celtic Folklore,* vol. 1, pp. 2–14.

267–8 *A Massariol . . . just won't do!'* From Gianbattista Bastanzi, *Le superstizioni delle Alpi Venete* (Treviso, 1888), p. 33.

268 *A Yugoslavian Mamalić . . . to do more damage.* From Pitré and Salomone-Marino, *Archivio,* vol. 20, p. 298.

268–9 *A small sea Maćić . . . for his stupidity.* From von Mailly, *Sagen,* p. 30.

269 *in your path!'* John C. Lawson, *Modern Greek Folklore and Ancient Greek Religion* (Cambridge, 1910), p. 150.

270 *a tortoise'.* Ibid., p. 156.

270–2 *A young man . . . saw her again.* From Schmidt, *Griechische Märchen,* p. 119.

272–3 *A young girl . . . in the village again.* From J. G. von Hahn, *Griechische und albanesische Märchen,* 2 vols (Leipzig, 1864), vol. 2, p. 80.

BIBLIOGRAPHY

Abbatius, Gian Alesio, *Il Pentamerone del Cavalier Giovan Battista Basile* (Naples, 1728).

Abjörnsen, P. and Moe, Jörgen, *Norwegische Volksmärchen* (Berlin, 1908).

Afanassiew, Alexander N., *Russische Volksmärchen* (Vienna, 1906).

—, *Russische Volksmärchen. Neue Folge* (Vienna, 1910).

Aichele, Walther, *Zigeuner Märchen* (Jena, 1926).

Alpenburg, Johann Nepomuk Ritter von, *Deutsche Alpensagen* (Vienna, 1861).

—, *Mythen und Sagen Tirols* (Zürich, 1857).

Alton, Giovanni, *Proverbi, Tradizioni ed Annedoti delle Valli Ladine orientali* (Innsbruck, 1881).

Amalfi, Gaetano, *Tradizioni ed Usi nella Peninsola Sorrentina* (Palermo, 1890).

Arndt, E. M., *Märchen und Jugenderinnerungen* (Berlin, 1818), part 1.

Babudri, F., *Fonti vive dei Veneto-Giuliani* (Milan, 1926).

Barrett, W. H., *Tales from the Fens* (London, 1963).

Barzaz-Briez, *Chants populaires de la Bretagne,* 2 vols (Paris, 1846).

Bastanzi, Gianbattista, *Le superstizioni delle Alpi Venete* (Treviso, 1888).

Bechstein, Ludwig, *Deutsches Sagenbuch* (Leipzig, 1853).

Benzel, Ulrich, *Volkserzählungen aus dem Oberpfälzisch-Böhmischen Grenzgebiet* (Münster, 1965).

Bernoni, Dom. Giuseppe, *Credenze popolari veneziane* (Venice, 1874).

—, *Leggende fantastiche popolari veneziane* (Venice, 1875).

Böckel, Otto, *Die Deutsche Volkssage* (Berlin, 1922).

Bødker, Laurits, *Dänische Volksmärchen* (Düsseldorf, 1964).

Bollettino storico lucchese (Lucca, 1935).

Bonomo, Giuseppe, *Studi Demologici,* (Palermo, 1970).

Bottiglioni, Gino, *Leggende e Tradizione di Sardegna* (Geneva, 1922).

—, *Vita Sarda* (Milan, 1925).

Brand, John, *Observations on the Popular Antiquities of Great Britain,* 3 vols (Detroit, 1969), vols 2 and 3.

Brewer's Dictionary of Phrase and Fable (London, 1962).

Briggs, K. M., *The Anatomy of Puck* (London, 1959).

—, *The Fairies in Tradition and Literature* (London, 1967).

Briggs, K. M. and Tongue, Ruth L., *Folktales of England* (London, 1965).

Bronzini, Giovanni, *Tradizioni popolari in Lucania* (Matera, 1953).

Bukowska-Grasse, Ewa and Koschmieder, Erwin, *Polnische Volksmärchen* (Düsseldorf, 1967).

Busk, R. H., *The Folk-Lore of Rome* (London, 1874).

Calvino, Italo, *Fiabe italiane,* 2 vols (Turin, 1956).

Campbell, J. F., *Popular Tales of the West Highlands,* 4 vols (Edinburgh, 1860–2).

Campbell, Rev. J. G., *Clan Traditions and Popular Tales of the Western Highlands,* vol. 5 of *Waifs and Strays of Celtic Tradition* (London, 1895).

Caravaggio, M. Giovanni Francesco Straporola da, *Le Piacevoli Notti* (Venice, 1551).

Choice Notes from Notes and Queries (London, 1859).

Christiansen, Reidar Th. and Stroebe, Klara, *Norwegische Volksmärchen* (Düsseldorf, 1967).

Colum, Padraic (ed.), *A Treasury of Irish Folklore* (New York, 1967).

Croker, Crofton, *Irische Elfenmärchen* (Frankfurt, 1966).

Curtin, Jeremiah, *Tales of the Fairies and of the Ghost World* (New York, 1971).

Dähnhardt, O., *Natursagen,* 6 vols (Leipzig, 1907–12).

Dawkins, R. M., *Modern Greek Folktales* (Oxford, 1953).

De Bhaldraithe, Tomás, *English–Irish Dictionary* (Baile átha Cliath, 1959).

Dégh, Linda, *Folktales of Hungary* (London, 1965).

Dorson, Richard M., *American Folklore* (Chicago, 1959).

Enciclopedia universal ilustrada (Barcelona, 1925).

Encyclopedia Italiana (Milan, 1932).

Eustachi-Nardi, Anna M., *Contributo allo studio delle tradizioni popolari marchigiani* (Florence, 1958).

Finamore, Gennaro, *Tradizioni popolari abruzzesi* (Turin, 1894).

The Folk-Lore Journal (London, 1888–), vols 1–7.

Fondi, Mario, *Abruzzo e Molise* (Turin, 1970).

Garnett, Lucy M. J., *Greek Folk Poesy,* 2 vols (London, 1896).

Geldart, Rev. E. Martin, *Modern Greek Folk Lore: the Tales of the People* (Leipzig, 1884).

Gigli, Giuseppe, *Superstizioni, pregiudizi e tradizioni* (Bologna, 1970).

Gill, W. W., *A Manx Scrapbook* (London, 1929).

—, *A Second Manx Scrapbook* (London, 1932).

Giovanni, Gaetano di, *Usi Credenze e Pregiudizi del Canavese* (Palermo, 1889).

Grande Dizionario Enciclopedico UTET (Turin, 1968).

La Grande Encyclopédie (Paris, 1900).

Graves, Robert, *The Greek Myths,* 2 vols (Edinburgh, 1957).

Gregory, Lady, *Visions and Beliefs in the West of Ireland,* 2 vols (London, 1920).

Grimm, Jacob, *Teutonic Mythology,* 4 vols (New York, 1966).

Grimm, Jacob and Wilhelm, *Fairy Tales* (London, 1954).

—, *Grimms Märchen,* 2 vols (Zürich, no date).

Guida all'Italia leggendaria misteriosa insolita fantastica, 2 vols (Milan, 1967).

Hahn, J. G. von, *Griechische und albanesische Märchen*, 2 vols (Leipzig, 1864).

Hallgarten, Paul, *Rhodos, die Märchen und Schwänke der Insel* (Frankfurt, 1929).

Halliwell, James Orchard, *Popular Rhymes and Nursery Tales* (London, 1859).

Henderson, William, *Notes on the Folk-lore of the Northern Counties of England and of the Borders* (London, 1879).

Hibbert, Samuel, *A Description of the Shetland Isles* (Edinburgh, 1822).

Hoffmann-Krayer, E. and Bächtold-Stäubli, Hanns, *Handwörterbuch des deutschen Aberglaubens*, 10 vols (Berlin, 1941).

Ilg, Bertha, *Maltesische Märchen und Schwänke*, 2 vols (Leipzig, 1906).

Jacobs, Joseph, *Celtic Fairy Tales* (London, 1895).

Johnson, R. Brimley (ed.), *A Book of British Ballads* (London, 1966).

Jones, Gwyn and Thomas (translators), *The Mabinogion* (London, 1966).

Jones, Rev. W. Henry and Kropf, Lewis L., *The Folktales of the Magyars* (London, 1889).

Jungbauer, Gustav, *Böhmerwald Märchen* (Passau, 1923).

Karadschitsch, Wuk Stephanowitsch, *Volksmärchen der Serben* (Berlin, 1854).

Karlinger, Felix, *Inselmärchen des Mittelmeeres* (Düsseldorf, 1960).

Keightley, Thomas, *The Fairy Mythology* (London, 1968).

Keller, Walter, *Italienische Märchen* (Jena, 1929).

Kennedy, Patrick, *Legendary Fictions of the Irish Celts* (London, 1866).

Kovács, Agnes, *Ungarische Volksmärchen* (Düsseldorf, 1966).

Krauss, Friederich, *Sagen und Märchen der Südslaven*, 2 vols (Leipzig, 1883).

—, *Volksglaube und religiöser Brauch der Südslaven* (Münster, 1890).

Kretschmer, P., *Neugriechische Märchen* (Jena, 1917).

Kuhn, Adalbert and Schwartz, W., *Norddeutsche Sagen, Märchen und Gebräuche* (Leipzig, 1848).

La Sorsa, Saverio, *Leggende di Puglia* (Bari, 1958).

—, *Tradizioni Popolari Pugliesi* (Rome, 1928).

Larousse, *New Larousse Encyclopedia of Mythology* (London, 1968).

Lawson, John C., *Modern Greek Folklore and Ancient Greek Religion* (Cambridge, 1910).

Leskien, August, *Balkanmärchen* (Jena, 1915).

Levi, Carlo, *Cristo si é fermato a Eboli* (Turin, 1958).

Luck, Georg, *Rätische Alpensagen* (Chur, 1935).

Machado y Alvarez, Antonio, *Biblioteca de las tradiciones populares españolas*, 10 vols (Seville, 1883).

MacInnes, Rev. D., *Folk and Hero Tales*, vol. 2 of Lord Archibald Campbell's *Waifs and Strays of Celtic Tradition* (London, 1890).

MacLellan, Angus, *Stories from South Uist* (London, 1961).

MacManus, D. A., *The Middle Kingdom* (London, 1975).

Mailath, Johann Grafen, *Magyarische Sagen, Märchen und Erzählungen*, 2 vols (Stuttgart, 1837).

Mailly, Anton von, *Sagen aus Friaul und den Julischen Alpen* (Leipzig, 1922).

Mannhardt, Wilhelm, *Antike Wald- und Feldkulte* (Berlin, 1877).

—, *Der Baumkultus der Germanen und ihrer Nachbarstämme* (Berlin, 1875).

—, *Antike Wald- und Feldkulte* (Berlin, 1877).

Manninen, Ilmari, 'Die Dämonischen Krankheiten in Finnischen Volks-aberglaube', in *Folklore Fellows Communications*, no. 45 (Helsinki, 1922).

Massignon, Geneviève, *Folktales of France* (London, 1966).

Maury, Alfred, *Croyances et Légendes du Moyen Age* (Paris, 1896).

Megas, Giorgios A., *Griechische Volksmärchen* (Düsseldorf, 1965).

—, *Folktales of Greece* (London, 1970).

Meier, Harri, *Spanische und Portugiesische Märchen* (Düsseldorf, 1940).

Menghin, Alois, *Aus dem deutschen Südtirol, Mythen, Sagen, Legenden und Schwänke, etc.* (Meran, 1884).

Merkelbach-Pinck, Angelika, *Lothringer Volksmärchen* (Düsseldorf, 1961).

Migliorini, Elio, *Veneto* (Turin, 1962).

Molony, Eileen, *Folk Tales from the West* (London, 1971).

Morandini, Giuseppe, *Trentino Alto Adige* (Turin, 1962).

Moser-Rath, Elfriede, *Deutsche Volksmärchen* (Düsseldorf, 1966).

Naake, John, *Slavonic Fairy Tales* (London, 1874).

Nilsson, Martin P., *A History of Greek Religion* (Oxford, 1963).

Nino, Antonio de, *Usi Abruzzesi*, 6 vols (Florence, 1879).

O'Faolain, Eileen, *Irish Sagas and Folk-Tales* (London, 1954).

O'Reilly, Edward, *An Irish–English Dictionary* (Dublin, 1864).

Ortutay, Gyula, *Ungarische Volksmärchen* (Berlin, 1957).

Ostermann, V., *La Vita in Friuli, Usi, Costumi, Credenze, Pregiudizi e Superstizioni Popolari* (Udine, 1894).

O'Sullivan, Sean, *Folktales of Ireland* (London, 1966).

—, *A Handbook of Irish Folklore* (London, 1963).

Pansa, Giovanni, *Miti, leggende e superstizioni dell' Abruzzo*, 2 vols (Sulmona, 1927).

Parry-Jones, D., *Welsh Legends and Fairy Lore* (London, 1953).

Partridge, Eric, *A Dictionary of Slang and Unconventional English*, 2 vols (London, 1961).

Pedroso, Consiglieri, *Portuguese Fairy Tales* (London, 1882).

Pitré, Giuseppe, *Novelle Popolari Toscane*, 2 vols (Rome, 1941).

—, *Usi e Costumi, Credenze e Pregiudizi del Popolo Siciliano*, 9 vols (Florence, 1944).

Pitré, Giuseppe and Salomone-Marino, S., *Archivio per lo studio delle tradizioni popolari*, 23 vols (Palermo, 1882–9).

Poli, Germano, *Venezia Tridentina* (Turin, 1927).

Porter, Enid, *Cambridgeshire Customs and Folklore* (London, 1969).

Prati, Angelico, *Folclore Trentino* (Milan, 1925).

Preindlsberger-Mrazović, Milena, *Bosnische Volksmärchen* (Innsbruck, 1905).

Radford, E. and M. A., *Encyclopaedia of Superstitions* (London, 1961).

Ralston, W. R. S., *Contes Populaires de la Russie* (Paris, 1874).

—, *The Songs of the Russian People* (London, 1872).

Ranke, Friedrich, *Die deutschen Volkssagen* (Munich, 1910).

Rehfues, P. J., *Gemählde von Neapel und seinen Umbebung* (Zürich, 1808), vol. 1.

Reiser, Karl August, *Sagen, Gebräuche und Sprichwörter des Allgäus*, 2 vols (Kempten, 1895).

Rhys, John, *Celtic Folklore*, 2 vols (Oxford, 1901).

Robertson, R. Macdonald, *More Highland Folk-Tales* (London, 1964).

—, *Selected Highland Folk-Tales* (London, 1961).

Rochholz, Ernst L., *Naturmythen* (Leipzig, 1862).

—, *Schweizersagen aus dem Aargau*, 2 vols (Aarau, 1956).

Róna-Sklacek, Elisabet, *Ungarische Volksmärchen* (Leipzig, 1909).

Rosa, Gabriele, *Dialetti, costumi e tradizioni nelle provincie di Bergamo e di Brescia* (Brescia, 1870).

Rua, Giuseppe, *Antiche Novelle in Versi* (Palermo, 1893).

Rubino, B. and Cocchiara, Giuseppe, *Usi e Costumi Novelle e Poesie del Popolo Siciliano* (Rome, 1924).

Salvator, Erzherzog Ludwig, *Märchen aus Mallorca* (Leipzig, 1896).

Savi-Lopez, Maria, *Alpensagen* (Stuttgart, 1893).

Schmidt, Bernhard, *Griechische Märchen, Sagen und Volkslieder* (Leipzig, 1877).

—, *Das Volksleben der Neugriechen und das Hellenische Alterthum* (Leipzig, 1871).

Schneller, Christian, *Märchen und Sagen aus Wälschtirol* (Innsbruck, 1867).

Schutz, Joseph, *Volksmärchen aus Jugoslawien* (Düsseldorf, 1960).

Schweizerisches Archiv für Volkskunde (Zürich, 1897–).

The Scottish National Dictionary (Edinburgh, 1953).

Sébillot, Paul, *Le Folk-Lore de France*, 4 vols (Paris, 1904–7).

Sikes, Wirt, *British Goblins* (London, 1973).

Sinistrari, Ludovico Maria, *Demoniality* (London, 1927).

Die Sonnentochter (Moscow, no date).

Soupalt, Ré, *Bretonische Märchen* (Düsseldorf, 1959).

—, *Französische Märchen* (Düsseldorf, 1963).

Stephens, James, *The Crock of Gold* (London, 1965).

—, *Irish Fairy Tales* (New York, 1962).

Strauss, Heinz A., *Psychologie und astrologische Symbolik* (Munich, 1971).

Stumme, Hans, *Maltesische Märchen* (Leipzig, 1904).

Temming, Rolf L., *Seemans-Sagen und Schiffer-Märchen* (Frankfurt, 1973).
Thiele, J. M., *Danmarks Folksagn*, 3 vols (Copenhagen, 1843).
Thorpe, Benjamin, *Northern Mythology*, 3 vols (London, 1852).
Tolkien, J. R. R., *The Tolkien Reader* (New York, 1966).
Tongue, Ruth L., *Forgotten Folk-Tales of the English Counties* (London, 1970).
—, *Somerset Folklore* (London, 1965).
Toschi, Paolo, *Romagna Solatia* (Milan, 1926).
Vasconcellos, J. Leite de, *Tradicões Populares de Portugal* (Porto, 1882).
Vernaleken, Theodor, *Österreichische Kinder- und Haus-Märchen* (Vienna, 1864).
Vidossi, Giuseppe, *Saggi e Scritti Minori di Folclore* (Turin, 1960).
Wardrop, Marjory, *Georgian Folk Tales* (London, 1894).
Webster, Wentworth, *Basque Legends* (London, 1879).
Wentz, Evans, *Fairy Faith in Celtic Countries* (London, 1975).
Wlislocki, Heinrich von, *Märchen und Sagen der Bukowiner und Siebenbürger Armenier* (Hamburg, 1891).
Wolf, Johannes Wilhelm, *Deutsche Märchen und Sagen* (Leipzig, 1845).
Wolff, C. F., *Ultimi Fiori delle Dolomiti* (Bologna, 1953).
Wright, Joseph, *The English Dialect Dictionary*, 6 vols (London, 1902).
Zaunert, Paul, *Deutsche Märchen aus dem Donaulande* (Jena, 1926).
—, *Deutsche Märchen seit Grimm* (Düsseldorf, 1964).
Zingarelli, N. and Vocino, M., *Apulia Fidelis* (Milan, 1926).
Zingerle, Ignaz, *Sagen aus Tirol* (Innsbruck, 1850).
Zingerle, Ignaz and Josef, *Tirols Volksdichtungen und Volksgebräuche*, 2 vols (vol. 1, Innsbruck, 1852, vol. 2, Regensburg, 1852).

INDEX OF NAMES

A name in CAPITALS indicates a separate entry in the main text, the numbers of the pages on which it occurs being in **bold** type. *Italics* denote pages containing illustrations.